My Walk

With My FATHER

And JESUS

Deacon John L. Smith, Ph. D.

Jupiter2Press

My Walk With My Father And Jesus is of religious content, and the human psychology

JUPITER4PRESS

ISBN-979-8-9915771-0-6

Published in the United States by Jupiter4Press in cooperation and arrangement with the author.

Jupiter4Press
Denton, Texas 76207-1734

Dedication

This book is dedicated to the creator of the Universe, my Father, and in memory of my wife, Kathy, my mother, Lillian, and my dad, John, and to my children, Lillian and John, and to my family and all my ancestors who made it possible for me to have life. I am eternally grateful for each of them and all their struggles to live a life that fostered children who, over time, made it possible for me to come into the world where I might know my Father. I am also grateful for all their extended families whose love, concern and support were helpful in their lives and the lives of their ancestors. Additionally, to all those who interacted with me that helped me become a voluntary servant for my Father.

Acknowledgments

I am grateful to several people whose support and encouragement helped me to overcome my fears by revealing those things about my relationship with my Father that is at the center of my existence. Of these are my mother and dad, the members of my family, my brother deacons, all those who my Father sent to me so that I might extend to them the love that my Father has for each of them, and a special heartfelt gratitude to Abe Schneider, Uncle Walter, Msgr. Barry, Archbishop Casey who ordained me, Dr. Randy Lumpp, Deacon Mark Salvato and Valerie Kreilick whose review of this book was very helpful. Michael and Mary Blackett whose encouragement and editing is appreciated, and most of all my ancestors whose willingness to protect and nurture their family, and their desire and dedication to life gave me the opportunity to also dedicate my life and to serve my God. It is on account of these and many others that I am a servant to my Father.

Author's Note

This book is about praying in a way that enables a lived encounter with the person of Jesus, those things in culture that are antithetical to having a lived encounter with the divine, meaning sin, paranormal attributes I have that is the origin for my discussion, spiritual gifts that are natural and how they are acquired. All of this opens the door for a discussion on human evolution as the source of how we discover the divine, how we develop non-instinctual or cognitive language and become conscious beings, and where spiritual attributes come from; that is, all from the psychological perspective of human instincts. This book is not a treatise on theology or any religious dogma but concerns human psychology as it relates to the above topics. A central tenet of my discussion is how becoming conscious beings opened the door to sin and that most sin is a product, in one way or another, of laws, dogmas, and ideologies.

The framework for my discussion is the conditions and circumstances of my life that were instrumental in how I discovered the divine, how these conditions were critical for the attributes, that for most people, are seen as paranormal, and how these events altered my life. These events, or incidents, revealed an extraordinary encounter with the divine. (I say incidents because I did not plan or seek any of them.) What I will report will seem impossible or even fanciful. That is the point, my Father is unequaled, and His desires for His people are beyond normal human experiences. Thus, the reason for this book, that you come to know the person of Jesus and His inexhaustible Love who will take you to the Father. However, just because we call such attributes paranormal, I demonstrate that they are within our instincts and are normal, rare but normal. I am not speaking coming to Jesus by believing in theological dogma but having a lived encounter with Him where your entire sensory apparatus declares that Jesus is alive and is real.

I encourage everyone to believe in God, for it is good and necessary for our wellbeing, but until a person has a completely sensory lived encounter with the divine, belief remains a belief. It is our senses that validate what is real and not a belief and, therefore, I am advocating for a sensory experience of the divine in one's life. When we have a lived experience of Jesus, who takes us to the Father, we begin to see the characteristics of the divine and how He interacts with us administering His grace and mercy, but most importantly how He forgives sin and shows us His infinite love for each of us.

I attempt to connect the reader to human instincts and to our sensory apparatus that provides humans with the only way we know that something is real, and that is the point of the book, everything in it is real and not ecclesiastically based, or for that matter even Christian even though this book is about Jesus. In Episodes 5-8 I demonstrate through visions the love that our Father has for us and how He gives His grace through Jesus to repentant souls. In Chapter 29 I offer a guide to praying in a fashion that can help facilitate a personal encounter with the person of Jesus.

Definitions

Consciousness: There are several different definitions for consciousness. The most well-known is a medical definition: a wakefulness and ability to be aware of our environment. This definition is appropriate for all living animals. Other understandings of consciousness are about mindfulness as related to being able to differentiate between themselves and the environment. I agree, but there is no distinction between an adult and a baby, who I contend is medically conscious but humanly unconscious. I hold that consciousness is a biproduct of cognitive or non-instinctual language and is the direct evolutionary result of identifying different gods with peoples outside of the group worshipping the god as a necessary way to identify the god. So, the first words of consciousness are nouns that carry within them adjectives and verbs. This dates human's conscious state about 25,000 years ago and will take another 12 to 15,000 years to become common across humanity. So, in modernity, a baby learns consciousness via language.

Divine: I use this term often to allow the reader to think about our instinctual discovery and drive to God. Our ancient ancestors experienced the divine and as civilization begins its evolution, the divine becomes God.

Ego-complex: The energetic center of psychological processes that unconsciously gives the organism identity; focus that interprets and organizes neurological processing that is created out of our sensorium. The ego-complex has passed through 50 million years of evolution with four distinct evolutionary stages.

Consciousness has six developmental stages that are characterized by their own similar yet different noetic way of thinking. I address two levels in this book; but the others are the foundation of who we are, but a discussion warrants its own book. The first level of consciousness is an oral noetic, followed by a literate noetic. Both are defined below.

Father: This term reflects my sensory experience of the divine. My encounters with the divine are about polio and pain. As a baby my pain was great, and I instinctively would go into what I called my place of peace where there was some being who gave me comfort, peace, and type of joy. I say joy because it was joyful not to be experiencing pain. Many years later I discovered that this unknown being was who I now call my Father.

gods: The use of the word "gods" is about the divine before and during early civilization. This was a time when humans, still unconscious, were spiritualizing the environment, and when humans began to become conscious beings, and during the early periods of civilization. There was no distinction between any component of the animal world and objects in the environment, including heavenly bodies, that were not being spiritualized. This resulted in the long process of functionally worshipping what was being spiritualized. This was carried over into civilizations but as gods.

Instincts: Instincts are an innate matrix that is part of the creation of the animal and set boundaries of behaviors that the animal can function within; they are immutable. All animals have and are governed by instincts. There is no function we have as a behavior or ability that isn't contained within our instincts. Knowledge of the divine, visions, and all manner of paranormal behaviors or abilities are contained within our instincts. We pray because it is an instinct; we worship that which we understand as being more powerful, even when that which we worship is man-made. This is where the quality of love comes from. It is a function of worship and energized by the instinct for survival. Our evolutionary trek began as a hominin over three million years ago and likely several hundred million years ago as mammals.

Energy, energic: This refers to psychological or mental energy that drives all behaviors. It is directly related to our senses, meaning sensory apparatus and it provides the brain with environmental data, within the body and outside of it.

Free will: This is the quality of our instincts that are most like the creator of the universe. This characteristic is the mechanism of how and why we sin. It is the central component of the Tree of Knowledge in the story of the fall of Adam and Eve in the Garden of Eden. It is also the reason it is so difficult to have encounters with the person of Jesus because our free will, as chosen to follow some aspects of laws, dogma, and ideologies, almost always unconsciously.

Jesus: Theologically, Jesus is the incarnation of an image and equal to God and the Holy Spirit. He was crucified, died, and rose from the dead on the third day, and is now seated at the right hand of the Father. My experience has shown me that Jesus has also become a symbol of the divine and is greater than what a religious dogma can contain. I have known people who did not believe in Jesus or whose religious background was of an Eastern religious doctrine who have the same psychological experiences as all Christians. Their religious beliefs don't seem to prohibit the effects of God's mercy, but sin and psychological beliefs seem to be the greatest obstacle to having a lived encounter with Jesus.

Noetic: Meaning the way we functionally think. There are two levels of noetics that I speak about in the book. **Oral**

noetic, that period after becoming conscious and language was without a fully phonetic alphabet. Children and people that do not have a fully phonetic alphabet, most of the world's population, have an oral noetic. And the last noetic to evolve is the **literate noetic** and is the product of fully phonetic alphabet and is the noetic of modernity. In a literate noetic, humans have evolved to have abstract thought, while in an oral noetic, abstractions are inferred. A very simple example is the oral noetic lives and thinks in a concrete world where eternity is inferred, while the literate noetic thinks of the eternal first and infers the concrete. This means that heaven, for the literate noetic, is an eternal place that is unknown but earthly images are used to describe it, and for the oral noetic, like Jesus had, heaven is a condition of earthly reality where righteousness is fully experienced, and the eternal is inferred.

Paleo-psychology: This is my attempt to apply psychological processes and energy to prehistoric and preconscious humans, as well as the ancestors of Homo sapiens. I approach this from the perspective of our instincts because our instincts are immutable, and its evolution within a matrix that defines who we are, what we are, and what will be.

Addendum
The Underpinnings of my Thesis

Orality and Literacy is a relatively new intellectual discipline founded about 50 years ago by Walter Ong, S.J. The discipline is generally applied to a wide spectrum of literary studies. I am unaware of its application to anthropological, paleontological, psychological, linguistic, neurological studies, which is the backbone of my thesis. Many people are unfamiliar with studies in Orality and Literacy, so, I am providing a quick overview as to how I am using the theories and ideas to my thesis.

Orality and Literacy is how humans think/reason. Ong noted that there is a difference in the manner those who wrote stories before the invention of the fully phonetic alphabet than those who wrote in a fully phonetic alphabet. He recognized that orality or sound has a different effect on the brain than what sight does. Sound creates an immediacy by interiorizing sound. This also has the effect of preventing abstract thinking, other than by inference. Sight creates a type of distance from the object, and, therefore, allows the brain to see beyond what a physical reality is. Those with an oral noetic live in a tangible reality where the spiritual is part of that world, earth bound. For example, the heavens, where the stars are, are part of their material reality, whereas for the literate orality the heavens can be a concrete reality as in astronomy or heaven as in the place where souls of the dead reside. When we look at the ancient Egyptians who had an oral noetic, and their understanding of the soul after death, we see the soul traveling in the world of the dead-on earth but unseen. Ong isolated the cause of this transformation of the way humans think to the invention of the fully phonetic alphabet by the Greeks in about 750 BC.

Western culture has long recognized there was a difference in the way humans think and account for it by suggesting that those who were educated in the West had what was called a Western philosophy, because in the East their philosophic understanding was very different, meaning within a concrete reality. Western philosophy is very abstract in its underpinnings and outcomes, while in the East everything is materialistic in its foundations and outcomes. What this means is that those with a Western philosophy have a literate noetic and those with an oral noetic have an Eastern philosophic view of reality. Further, the implications of this is the peoples with an oral noetic are those in cultures that are not educated in a fully phonetic alphabet, meaning most of the world's population. I also suggest that this is true in modernity with children, and they pass through each noetic in which they live.

Ong also postulated that because sight and sound directly affect the manner humans think that the senses play an important role in the manner humans think. The role of the senses is what he calls the Sensorium, a type of psychological description of neurological processes of sensory information of the external and internal world in which the species lives. So, the sensorium is the neuro/psychological process by which all information enters the brain, be it in concrete reality or from a spiritual realm, be it real or not.

I suggest that all human behaviors function within our instincts. This means that no behavior or psychic encounter is outside of our instincts. Our DNA determines all that we are and to think that we can become something outside of our instincts is impossible. In like manner our instincts function within our DNA and, therefore, all behaviors and thought processes are contained within our instincts. There are many things that exist that we are unaware of because they are outside of what we can perceive. However, with a literate noetic we can infer that things exist and then develop a tool that can allow us to become aware of them. This is not possible with an oral noetic.

I differentiate between awareness of environs and being conscious of our environment. All animals have awareness of their environment, but only humans can assess their relationship to the environment, and, therefore, a conscious being. This is unlike a medical definition of consciousness which can respond to outside stimuli. I will demonstrate that consciousness is a function of a mutated hippocampus, the evolution of instinctual language to a non-instinctual language that creates consciousness.

All human behaviors are affected by whether a species is conscious and the manner that they think/reason. Any species that is not conscious will behave and think about their environs via their instincts, and if unable to respond they are unconscious. So, an infant is a conscious being when a medical definition is applied but is an unconscious being in my definition. I also suggest that a person who is an unconscious being is unable to think, meaning to assess their environs.

I apply my theory to the evolution of humans over about three million years and demonstrate how humans become conscious beings, discovered gods, and why we are driven to the divine. I explore why we no longer are with the gods as our ancient ancestors were. This leads me to explore why we are separated from gods and using my thesis I discuss sin, or separation from the gods. Sin is not theological but evolutionary and is part of the human condition for millions of years and imbued into our instincts, although without being conscious of it until the development of a pre-oral noetic about 25,000 years ago. I demonstrate where sin comes from, what it is, what its effects are, and how sin is overcome. My theory demonstrates God is real, sin is real, and that it is God's desire for us to live in communion with him. I will also demonstrate that Jesus is real and a tool of our Father to help us come into union with Him in the here-and-now. No aspect of my theory is theological but is based completely on the human condition.

EPISODE 1
How do Humans Know about the Divine?

1

Our Spiritual Nature – Overview

From a psychological and instinctual perspective, Jesus is not Christian, Muslim, or any other religious doctrine but He is the personification of the creator of the universe and the divine person of humanity who is above all human laws, dogmas, and ideologies. He will come to any person who calls upon Him, regardless of their belief system, provided, if for no more than an instant, the person overcomes how they are imbued with worldly laws, dogmas, and ideologies. These are the things that separate us from the divine in this life, and the divine will not move against a person's free will, so the person must have the unrelenting desire to be with Jesus regardless of his or her beliefs. It only takes a small opening into the instinctual depths of the person's heart, the instinctual heart that has always and will always seek the Father. After the fullness of time, His son Jesus, His living icon of the Father, always takes us to the Father. But how does this come about?

Over 40 years I have had the greatest of all privileges: to see, touch, and hear the voice of the creator of the universe. What an honor, totally unworthy for such a distinction, but one I am so blessed to receive, and I know that the divine wants to have similar encounters with every person. If I am asked if I have ever seen, touched, and heard the creator of the universe, the lie detector will affirm that I have, but I will also say, I am imbued with laws, dogmas, and ideologies that make it very difficult for me to be with Him. This greatest of blessing is also the source of my greatest sin, not publicly witnessing the presence of Jesus in a fallen world because of my fears of being ostracized, laughed at, ridiculed, and humiliated. This is something that I finally decided to put up with, but I was not willing to allow others to attack me while my wife was alive, and my children were young. But now all that has changed. My children have their own lives and my wife, who died three years ago, will not have to struggle with such attacks.

This book is not about theology, or any religious dogmas, but a book about human sensory and emotional experiences of the divine, specifically Jesus, with whom I participated. This is my testimony of the encounters with what I identify as the divine. Everything inscribed on the pages of my testimony about my Father, Jesus, and the providential guidance and intervention of the Holy Spirit are my observations and commentary on events that occurred throughout my life. When I speak of the divine, it is not a theological statement, but psychological and emotional testimony of my spirit crying out that what I have experienced was something that I perceived as being greater than I am, more powerful, and a love that I cannot even imagine as being humanly possible. Therefore, the reason that I claim my Father, Jesus, and a spirit that is invisible but is psychologically and emotionally perceived as a person, but whose power, love, and peace is beyond what humans have achieved and, therefore, why I identify them as divine. Nor am I saying that what I claim is the divine can be

[4]

proven, but it is a matter of faith, but faith based on human experience which is the only way humans know what is real.

From my perspective, the Spirit I call my God is the creator of the universe and is based on my experiences of immeasurable power that I interpret as being a person without beginning and without end. My experiences of Jesus and what seems to be my Father's spirit that I call the Holy Spirit and seemingly knows and understands all things, which is the way that the heart of every person is known to the Father. I also testify that all those who experienced the person of Jesus through His visitation to them also and instinctively knew that the one they encountered was Jesus. This is critically important and what separates this book from a theological interpretation. Those who encountered the person of Jesus knew who He was not by faith, but by their senses and their instinctual identification of the person of Jesus.

Further, some of those I report as having an encounter with Jesus did not believe or have any relationship with Jesus prior to their encounter with Jesus but knew about Him. Even in these cases the person knew in the depths of their being that the person they met was Jesus and that He is divine. What do I mean by the divine? From our instinct's perspective, the divine is the spiritual nature of Homo sapiens and the divine is within our instincts, as well as everything. The drive to discovery is the drive to discover and be with the divine. Religions are very important, but they tend towards promulgating intellectual truths while shying away from lived encounters with the divine. From my perspective theology is the intellectual study of God, which I believe is wonderful and most helpful for people coming to God, while encountering the divine via our senses is experientially knowing the divine. It is like believing that I can go into space versus being in space, a big difference.

[5]

Many people I prayed with I never saw again so I don't know how their lives changed or if those who encountered Jesus fully accepted Him as divine or not, but I do know that the encounter was life changing because of how Jesus healed their mind, body, and/or spirit. Of those I continued to contact, I know their relationship with Jesus continued to grow long after their encounter. Even those who rejected God's love knew who they were rejecting, very sad, but I am sure that God was always ready to welcome them into His heart when they were ready. Even after death the love and His nature continue, but the divine never revealed to me in all my encounters with Him that He forces Himself on anyone, what I interpret as human freewill, a characteristic of the divine.

2

The gods
Complex and Controversial

This is a very complex and controversial topic. When I consider the ramifications and implications of humanity's search and discovery of the gods, it really deserves its own book, but the topic is essential to my discussion on prayer and my relationship with my Father. In this episode the discussion will provide a brief overview of how humans came to be the only animals on the planet that achieved self-awareness and to recognize they are different from all other species of animals. The ability to make tools, to travel across the planet and into space and another celestial body, and to communicate in a variety of ways and across vast distances are just a few examples. I will offer how humans discover the divine and from the human instinctual perspective where the divine came from, where paranormal gifts come from and why we worship and pray. These questions have resided in the hearts of humanity from time immemorial and using the encounters of others and myself with the person of Jesus as one of the sources of my research, I will attempt to provide insights into these questions. As noted above, these are complex and very difficult topics to cover and far beyond the scope of this book, so in this episode, I will try to layout an overview.

How do we know there is a divine?

Our culture and the cultures around the world, save communistic governments, all hold that there is a divine being. However, as much as I wish all peoples would believe in the divine, I also pray that all would have a lived experience of the divine where they have a sensory encounter that tells them the divine is real. But for almost everyone in the world we have a belief in varying degrees. The only way we know anything exists is by our senses. Therefore, something that is intellectually proposed might be true but must be revealed in such a way that our senses verify that it is real. It must also be noted that simply because our senses tell us something is there, doesn't mean that our interpretation of what we sense is correct. For example, in the political realm a politician or political party may tell us what we see, and experience is not what our senses tell us is true, but what the political jargon wants it to be is what is true, contrary to what our senses reveal. This is also common with laws, dogmas, and ideologies. We are always better off to trust that which provides data, our senses, and not interpretation. The same is true about the divine. It is our sensory apparatus that has revealed to humanity that there is a divine. It was never an intellectual idea that was promulgated by elites who sought power over people. It was the people's experience, or better to say, lived encounters, with the divine that began a journey of worshipping the divine beginning at least 50,000 plus years ago. But humans and our ancestors have encountered the divine, from within our instincts, for many millions of years, because the instinct for the divine has been part of the human condition from the beginning.

As humans were beginning the arduous journey of becoming conscious, it was their encounters with objects and animals that projected power that first made them realize they were special in their world. These were functionally sensory experiences and part of our instincts for the gods as we see everywhere humans lived the same phenomena. Humans were becoming more interactive with the images of the divine by beginning to bury their dead, placing symbolic features on rock walls, and producing beautiful pictures of the animals of power, and those critical to their survival, as if to acknowledge their importance to them. These are all sensory applications of the unfolding image of the divine, and for tens of thousands of years occurred without law, dogma, or ideology. They do not become part of the picture of humans discovering the gods until the advent of common or non-instinctual languages that doesn't begin to come about until roughly 25,000 years ago but not fully incorporated into the human condition until about 10,000 years ago.

Humanity's first encounters with the divine

As the images of the divine become more prominent and exert more power in the lives of our ancestors beginning over 50,000 years ago, they began to worship the animals and objects of power. The psychic energy for this was very powerful and was directly linked to the instinct for survival. Humans were still functionally unconscious, meaning unable to distinguish that they were different from the objects and animals they encountered during their life. This was the psychological state of humans and their ancestors for millions of years. By the time Homo sapiens evolved about 200,000 years ago, humans' encounter with animals and objects psychologically carried with it a spiritual sense to what they encountered. The spiritual instinct carried within the need to worship the animal or object, all from an unconscious manner, like the way a baby instinctually

[9]

knows his mother or the way to reach out for food. The spiritual nature of reality was functionally the effects of the psychological function of intuition that is also critical in the creation of tools.

Ancient ritual

Don't think of the manner of worship as the manner we worship in modernity, but more like a family coming together in the evening and drumming and chanting in their instinctual language and entering a trance-like state that united the person or even the family into the spirit of the object or animal they were worshipping, meaning the object of their focus. Some research suggests that hunter gatherers would become entranced and, in the process, would spiritually become the animal they hunt to know how to better pursue the animal in the hunt. Their lived knowledge of animals gave them great insights into the animals' nature. Because of the spiritual connection, there became a oneness with animals and respect and thankfulness for their life that allows the human to have food, and eventually to use the skin, bone, and other parts of the animal for tools that aided their survival.

All this took place over tens of thousands of years before humans became conscious beings or had common or non-instinctual language. To achieve a trance-like state was much easier because the people had not yet become aware of their state of normal animal awareness. The type of awareness our ancestors had prior to becoming conscious beings was no different than our cousins, the chimpanzees, but we had tools that greatly provided early humans with a perspective of reality that was much different.

Our ancestors spiritualizing the world

As regards becoming conscious beings, it was the psychic energy that was becoming greater and greater that was being stimulated by the increasing spiritual engagement of animals, objects and tools that provided more energy being diverted to the spiritual interaction between humans and their environment through ritual. It is this perspective that was opening the functional aspect of the brain and its unique nature that allowed the power of animals, nature, and objects to become spiritualized, and the ability to emotionally connect to these things, allowing for them to emote a hierarchy of power, although not consciously. Our ancestors lived and functioned in a dream-like state that allowed them to encounter the environment and to spiritualize it, as if they were living in two worlds, the physical world, and a spiritualized world.

In the lived experience of our ancient ancestors the lion was more powerful than most predators, but a crocodile was even more formidable, and the eagle that was not as strong was able to fly above dangers and, therefore, more capable. This example is but one of the ways our ancestors spiritualized the environment. This was not an intellectual exercise but emotional and thus carried with it emotional or psychic energy. It was also the beginning of abstract thought processes, but such thinking would not fully develop until about the 7th century B.C.E. This process evolved over a long period and would lead early civilization to have multiple gods that became environmental functionaries. All of nature was being emotionally placed into a hierarchy including animals that seemingly were deadly to humans especially those very subtle and cunning about the way they interacted with people; like snakes that kill but don't consume the person, like other predators. Snakes for millions of years would be avoided at all costs and is the

[11]

reason the serpent is identified as the evil one in the Garden of Eden.

Worshipping the gods

The functional and fully sensory worship of the gods became more and more complex and typically the leader of the clan would be the primary figure at how and when worship would take place. This was unfolding at least 50,000 years ago; with indications such behavior goes back to the beginnings of Homo sapiens over 200,000 years ago. And, because human relationship with the heaven was so imbued into the psyche, peace and power rituals began to gravitate around celestial events that were seasonally repeated. Even without being conscious and functioning completely out of our instincts, our ancestors knew very well the heavens and the seasons of the year. Remember they lived outdoors and under the stars for millions of years, only beginning to have permanent shelter, as in caves, only if available and to remain there for any period was dependent on the availability of game, roots and berries, and the like. More permanent structures would have to wait until neo-lithic times and the invention of agricultural and domestication of animals, and the formative period for language, which is the functional result of spiritualizing the world and worshipping the gods. The development of permanent structures didn't require our ancestors to follow the migratory patterns of animals but required other development of tools that allowed for a new evolution of Homo sapiens to slowly unfold.

It was during this period, beginning at the end of the last Ice Age that started about 25,000 to 35,000 years ago that a major transition was beginning to take place. Humans were slowly being transformed via their increasing interaction with the spiritualization of the environment and

[12]

heaven, animals, and physical objects that were becoming psychologically energized by the projection of spiritual energy to allow for more and more worship and as the climate was beginning to warm, survival became easier. It would take about another 10,000 to 25,000 years for the Neo-lithic period to get its start and transform humans to become civilized. Besides the invention of agriculture and domestication, it was a time when larger communities began to evolve, and the spiritual reality of the environment was now beginning to be worshipped by building what we call monuments to the gods. Now the sounds of the ritual of the family were becoming part of monument construction to enhance reverberating sounds that, to the people, seemed as though the gods were speaking to them, and incorporated with astrological connections to the cycles of the seasons, and their worshipping of the animals and environment and the memorializing of their ancestors these mega-lithic sites became spiritually powerful, enticing peoples from very distant places to come to the places of the gods and for building larger and larger sites. The coming together of diverse peoples created the need for common language to communicate what needed to be done in building sites and how they would be built, as well as who and how worship would take place. The first words, I suggest, were nouns that also carried within the word, adjective and verb. So, the word for a specific god, say Og, would inform the hearer, who, what, when, and how Og would be worshipped. By time I am speaking about seasonal and celestial.

Creating non-instinctual language

The process of creating conscious or non-instinctual languages would take a long time, perhaps 10,000 years or longer in some places. It was the process of creating non-instinctual language that simultaneously brought the species

[13]

out of the darkness of instinctual existence into the light of the world. As each generation's language became stronger, so did the light of a new world become brighter. The gods were becoming more individuated and greater and greater ceremonies were being created to worship their gods. It also must be noted that what we call sin was simultaneously coupled with the progression of language that reflected how, if the gods failed to provide what they were endowed to do, the people and particularly the leaders, could account for the mishaps of the gods.

These sinful behaviors on the part of the people generally revolving around improper worshipping practices, which means that how, why, when, and where the people worshipped were very important because worship was about a lived encounter with the spirit of the object being worshipped, and if there was no encounter, the reason was about sin. It is important to remember that our ancestors had a lived encounter with their gods, not a belief system as we do today, but when the people did not have an encounter with the divine, they were in a state of sin and reconciliation had to be effected. This went back over many tens of thousands of years to families worshipping of the gods.

But sin was already instinctual within the species, meaning what is good and evil or bad. This was established over millions of years of behaviors related to survival. Behaviors that provided survival were infused as good, and behaviors that did not promote survival became encoded in our instincts as evil. In modernity, what is evil is that which is not, nor does not support survival. I will have more to say about sin below.

Linked to the evolution of non-instinctual language, the worship of the gods, and building places to memorialize and worship the gods and ancestors was allowing more and more people to come together resulting in small communities

[14]

becoming villages, and then cities that would become what we call civilization; the first of which was about 4 to 5,000 years ago. This minimal discussion of how we discovered the gods, became a spiritual people, created worship systems, language, consciousness, and civilization is important to my overall discussion of prayer.

The mutation of the brain

Above I spoke about how the brain has special qualities that allow the function of the brain to be the primary reason Homo sapiens become conscious beings. All animals have instinctual language but why are humans the only animal that has non-instinctual language? All primates have a bicameral hippocampus, and it functions in the same way for all primates, except for us. Why? The reason is the mutation of the left hippocampi of the bicameral hippocampus in our brain. When we examine brain structure, we find that the difference is primarily in the hippocampus, which is part of the cerebellum, connected to the temporal lobe and is associated with memory, emotions, language, and helps with the encoding of environmental data, the sensorium. The right hippocampi function the same in all primates, including humans. It is the left hippocampi that functions differently in Homo sapiens. Simply, it processes the information from the sensorium in a linear manner instead of spatially as in the right hemisphere. This is critical for the development of conscious language, which is the way we become conscious beings, and know God.

As I said, all primates other than humans have only non-instinctual language. They have no gods, and the world they live in is without consciousness, and metaphorically dark. They live completely within their instincts and without sin. This mutation occurred about three million years ago. Further, this mutation allowed for the functional ability to

[15]

exercise free will, and is central to human psychology, specifically the ego-complex, and the ability to utilize intuition in ways that our primate cousins are unable to do.

What I laid out in Chapter 2 probably sounds overpowering and confusing. What I want the reader to come away with is: First, the human condition is complicated, and has been evolving for a very long time, millions of years as a primate, and hundreds of millions of years as a mammal; and, secondly, Homo sapiens are the only primate that have a hippocampus whose left chamber of the hippocampus processes sensory information in a linear fashion while all other primates process sensory information spatially. This has allowed for non-instinctual language to evolve as well as consciousness, the ability to differentiate ourselves from all other objects and beings.

EPISODE 2
The Invitation

3

How I Came to Discover there is a Divine Person

The divine intervention into my life

I was born with Rickets, a disease of the body's inability to adequately absorb Vitamin D, resulting in soft bones. It seemed that I lived on cod liver oil until I was nine years old. I can still taste it and it is likely the reason I don't like fish. There was a concern I would not live, and the medical staff asked my mother if she wanted me to receive the Last Rites. My mother, who was a non-practicing Catholic, said yes. I survived only to receive the Last Rites again 12 months later because of an allergic reaction to coal dust from the burning of coal for industry and heating homes in St. Louis, MO. The doctors told my parents I would die within a matter of days, and that my only hope was to be taken out of any place that burned coal, but they also thought I would not survive traveling. My parents had just moved from California several weeks earlier, where I was born, to St. Louis to be with their families and to be reunited with their daughter. She had been living with my dad's sister and husband for the decade of the 1930's because my aunt and uncle worked for a wealthy family and, unlike most people, were not financially affected by the depression. Within several days of being reunited with my sister and being told to get me out of the polluted air, my parents had to decide what to do about my sister. They decided to take me and her back to California that very day. The only way to get there was to drive or take a train but because of the expense of traveling, and because they needed their car, the only option was to drive. After several days they got as far as Amarillo, TX when the car broke down and my parents didn't have enough money to get it repaired. My mother had received a card from the medical staff when they left the hospital. She thought it was a card wishing for me to get well. She opened it while they were trying to figure out what to do about the repair of the car. The note said, "we are sorry that Johnny died, and we know you don't have much money and so the staff all donated money for Johnny's funeral." They used the funds for my funeral to fix the car and return to California. In those days the Las Angelus region was mostly agricultural, and the air was clean. Years later the polluted air forced me and my family to move to Denver because I contracted COPD, a disease related to my allergic reaction to coal dust.

Shortly after arriving in Pasadena, CA, where my parents lived before going to St. Louis, I was stricken with polio. I was 14 months old and again received the Last Rites, but I was very fortunate. In those days about half of those who got polio died, and about 25% went into an iron lung, the remaining, like me, were paralyzed to some degree. In my case I was paralyzed from the waist down, primarily on my right side, but was affected from the shoulders down. Over time I recovered enough to become normal, or what I considered to be, but only after a significant amount of therapy and focus on rebuilding my body.

My sister was born 10 years before me and shortly after her birth my mother contracted Multiple Sclerosis, a disease where the immune system attacks the protective covering of nerves. My mother had a rare form of the disease, and she was unable to carry a pregnancy to full-term, except for me. When I was born, as I noted, I was born with Rickets and an allergic condition with air pollution that I still have, but not as bad as when I was younger, likely the results of my mother's Multiple Sclerosis. These conditions almost took my life on three occasions in the first 14 months of my life, and I believe that my Father intervened to save my life. By intervened I mean in some way it was in accord with my will, perhaps the instinctual will to survive, but I don't believe God just chose me to be saved.

I knew my Father intervened to alert me to the need for heart surgery when I was 75 years old. Using the symptoms of Post Polio Syndrome got me to a cardiologist who could not find anything wrong with my heart, but when I asked him to do a heart catheterization, it revealed an immediate need for five bypasses, or I would die within the month. I had a rare heart condition, and I would have never known I needed heart surgery if I didn't have Post Polio Syndrome. This event was the impetus for me to reflect on my early life and came to believe that my Father also intervened when I was born, almost died from Rickets, then coal dust, and when I contracted polio. I also recognized that he was there when I was in the Air Force and wounded, and when the medics arrived the last words I heard before passing out was, "he is going to die." I was in the hospital for nine months and recovery took four and a half years.

Discovering the divine

I am most indebted to my Father for the gift of sicknesses and injuries and in particularly the disease of polio that introduced me to the divine who I eventually called "my Father." He provided me with his peace, joy, and comfort that sustained me through the pain of polio, then and now. I contracted polio at a young age, and because I was only one year old, I did not know anything about the divine. By the time I was three years old, I emotionally knew the love and care of my mother, dad and a nurse friend of the family who helped me to walk again. But there was a fourth person with whom I emotionally identified, and it was this person who gave me the peace and joy amid great pain and suffering. Emotionally, I did not know this person, but unlike the others who I could see, this person was only there when my pain was severe and unmanageable. By the age of seven or eight, I was walking reasonably well but at night my pain levels were severe, and my relief was heat. Some days nothing helped so I turned to that space in my mind where I experienced peace and freedom from the pain. Whenever I entered my place of peace, I found the person I thought provided my freedom from pain. This unknown and unseen person was very familiar because he was there as far back as I could remember. I had an emotional memory of him being there. This person knew my suffering and pain better than anybody and was extremely compassionate and loving. I didn't tell anyone about this person until I was seven or eight years old, as I thought it was normal and everybody knew about him. When I said something to my parents, they were as baffled as I was. When I was in my late teens, I began to wonder why I had this unknown person helping me with pain, and why I never heard that anybody else had someone who helped them with their pain. I especially wondered about my mother with her Multiple Sclerosis as it was very painful for her.

Eventually, I wanted to know who this person was, and it became the impetus for my search for this invisible person. When I was 40 years old, he introduced himself to me as my Father. I need to point out that his introduction of himself was an audible voice that spoke to me in the same manner a friend has a conversation with me. This was a transformative experience that revealed who he wanted me to be, my path. And then, slowly over the next forty years he revealed to me via his son Jesus my Father's characteristics that painted a picture of who he is, as well as who Jesus is. A picture of that is, I pray, that this book does justice to by revealing sensory and functional experiences of the divine revealing to me who my Father and who Jesus are. What I mean by functionally revealing who my Father and Jesus are is what my emotions and senses tells me is true.

My place of peace and my Father

My life is filled with pain and that is the primary way that my Father introduced himself to me when I was under two years of age. One might think it was because I didn't have cognitive abilities at such a young age that I was unable to know the divine. But as I have pointed out, an infant knows love experientially through his mother's arms. He can't say what he experiences but if an infant does not experience the love of a person, studies show the infant will either die or be severely emotionally damaged. We are created to receive love and to give love. My parents loved me, but when the pain of polio was severe, I began to withdraw from the world and go into my interior space where I met my Father. This didn't occur immediately but over time I emotionally found peace. However, it wasn't until I was six or seven years old that I began to recognize that there were times when I had severe pain and was unable to do anything about it, other than what my parents did to help relieve the pain with heat and massage. It was at those times when I would seek my place of peace, that I began to call my Father because it seemed to me that there was a

[23]

person in my place of peace. From the age of eight years old to as far back as I could remember, I cried myself to sleep. But there were times I naturally seemed to mentally go into my mind and seek my Father and his peace.

The outward search for my Father

My parents did not go to church, and my mother as a non-practicing Catholic never spoke about God, nor did my dad who had a protestant belief. I was in my thirties before I knew I had been baptized a Roman Catholic as an infant. When I was about seven years old, I overheard my parents and their friends speaking about God and wondered if such a person or being existed because I never knew about God. As I wondered about it, I seemed to be drawn towards searching for this God. When I was seven and for about the next eight years I would periodically go to different churches because this was where people said God was. On Sunday mornings, at times, I would go out to play but went to a Lutheran Church several miles away from home. I would walk to the church and back home, and my parents never knew where I was going. I never discovered the God I heard my parents and their friends speak of. I would discover years later that the friends were part of the family and were members and ministers of the Salvation Army.

By the time I was 15 years old, I had gone to or researched many churches. I read the entire bible, Book of Mormon and went to their church, materials on many protestant faith systems, and non-Christian beliefs like Hinduism, Buddhism, Spiritualism, Islam as well as Taoism, Shintoism, and Confucianism. I attended the Presbyterian, Lutheran, Methodist, Church of God, and Evangelical churches, and the Church of Religious Science. None of these gave me a sensory experience of Love or Peace. They all had attributes that were positive, but none met what I was looking for and I lost interest in them. What was most important to me was finding my Father, but none of this research filled me with what I was looking for. When I was older, I got a degree in Religious Studies, and I continued my study of religions but now I was interested in why so many different religions, if there is but one God. My parents were never aware that I had gone to any church nor that I was searching for my Father.

As I pointed out above, I tended to be rather independent and would go places and do things on my own. This was true as I began my search for my Father, that is still going on, but now I have greater insights and sensory experiences that provide me with a name and characteristics of my Father.

My Confirmation as a Roman Catholic

My interest in God is very important to me. When I was 14 years old two of my friends and I went shopping in another town and we hitchhiked to and from our shopping. On our way home an evangelical preacher picked us up and began to preach about Jesus and wanted us to accept Jesus as our savior. We thought he was a little eccentric, so we asked him to let us out. He pulled over to the side of the road and gave each of us a wallet size card wanting us to check the box that said. "I accept Jesus as my savior." My two friends that got out first took the card and threw it to the ground. When I read the card, there was another box that said, "I dedicate my life to God." I checked both boxes and to this day I carry that card in my wallet. The man's name was on the card. It was Abe Schneider.

Ten years later I was married to a strongly practicing Roman Catholic. After we were married 10 years, and after a multi-year and in-depth investigation into the Roman Catholic Church, I was confirmed. But I must say, like all

[25]

the religious beliefs, the Catholic Church also didn't provide me with an encounter with my Father, but I came to the belief that I was to continue my search for my Father. Although, before I became a deacon in the Church, I had several encounters with my Father that were very spiritually powerful that affected me, and many others.

The Confirmation was at the Cathedral and when I got to the church for the ceremony, I did not have a sponsor. There was a man standing there, who I did not know, who was going to be the sponsor for another person. He volunteered to be my sponsor as well. The priest standing there agreed and allowed me to be confirmed, for which I was grateful. He introduced himself and his name was Abe Schneider, the same name as the evangelist that asked me to accept Jesus as my savior. This was very serendipitous to me, especially because the name Abe Schneider is Jewish. I understood this to be my Father telling me that I was on the right track, on the path.

My continued interest in finding my Father

I still had an overwhelming desire to know who my Father is, the person who took my pain away and gave me peace and love. I say person because my experience with the one who comforts me was emotionally perceived as a person, except I could not see him. This led me on a great journey of discovery searching for the one who is the source of my peace and joy while suffering with physical pain. This is an ongoing journey for me. Also, while I searched for the person at the center of alleviating my pain, I became lost and off the path many times, that I considered making my quest more difficult. I will say more about this journey throughout this book. However, note how my search for the divine is totally functional and predicated on the senses, and not about any law, dogma, or ideology about the divine.

[26]

My research into the Roman Catholic Church also led me down a path of Western history, the Jewish faith and history, as well as Roman, Egyptian, and Middle Eastern history. To help satisfy that interest, I earned a Bachelor's Degree in Religious Studies. But then I had more questions than answers. All Western religions are at their core based upon Greek philosophy, so I got a Bachelor's Degree in Philosophy but again I had more questions and no answers as to the identity of my Father. Much of my studies seem to indicate that people seem to interpret the same data in different ways. Why? So, I thought I needed a degree in psychology, which I got, plus I was awarded a Master's Degree in the Psychology of Typology, and then my Doctorate in Psychology. This led me to an interest in our ancestors and why they also sought the gods, even back 200,000 years. I still have great interest in this; particularly, if we accept the idea that God is unchangeable. So, my search for my Father is no different than the search for the divine of my ancestors for many thousands of years. I am in good company.

I am very interested in our Stone Age ancestors and their discovery of the gods, as well as where humans came from, our evolution, and why we are different from other primates when our DNA is almost identical. Why do we believe in gods, the divine, and think there is life after death? When did humans first begin to believe in such things? These are the questions that humans have asked from time immemorial, and I can assure you that I can't answer them; however, the answers will not be found in the ideologies of modernity, but we will have to enter, with the mindset of our ancestors, at least as much as possible, and explore what human senses have to say about the gods, which I outlined above.

[27]

4

Coming to Know the Divine and how we become Separated

How do people know anything?

The only way we know anything is via our senses and is the hinge point of my thesis. If our senses do not perceive something for us, it does not exist. So, we see light from the sun but do not see an infrared spectrum of the visible light. How then do we know about infrared light? The answer is tools. A tool is anything created by a human that is used for a specific purpose to do something that allows our senses to perceive its purpose. Stone in nature naturally has rounded edges and is not suitable for cutting and chopping. For example, the first tool, a chopper, created about 2.5 million years ago gave hominin an advantage in food preparation and procurement, and over time a methodology on how to develop other tools. In other words, the chopper as a tool allowed hominins to perceive a new reality, one where nature could be modified. This, over a very long period, will modify the brain, both in size and function. I suggest that the impetus for transition from one species to the next are tools because they give us power over nature. Tools create pressure on the brain to make space for greater and greater tools that continually change the world. Tools can only be created that are structured and function within the parameters of our instincts.

It is important to understand that without tools, that which we cannot perceive with our senses remains unknown. Even though there are things that we cannot detect with our senses, we can postulate that something exists because we see with our senses that it influences something. For example, a person can receive a sunburn even when it is a cloudy day, meaning that getting a sunburn is not directly related to visible sunlight, but that something else is the cause of sunburn. We don't get a sunburn at night, so, there is something about sunlight, of which we are unaware, that causes people to get a sunburn. This is the impetus for scientists to explore visible sunlight and to see if there are other qualities of light that we don't know about. For this to happen we need to invent tools that can give us the information we need to know about sunlight and reveal what is invisible to become known via a tool. This is a very rough example of the discovery of ultraviolet light or radiation.

Jesus, the Father's tool for humanity

Jesus is my Father's tool that reveals my Father's existence better than any other tool. But any tool cannot be entirely intellectual or speculative but must be validated through our senses and functional. So, belief in Jesus is wonderful, but unless we encounter him and the encounter is validated by our senses, Jesus remains a belief and outside of functional emotional faith. The purpose of this book is to encourage all people, regardless of their faith system, to have a lived encounter with the person of Jesus, who is the tool created by the divine to reveal his nature to us. Not something that is psychosomatic or based on theological dogmas, but an encounter in which the person can feel the

[29]

warmth of his hand and hear his voice speaking to you. This goes far beyond any belief system and reveals the divine is a real person, eternal, and intimately lives within each person.

In the first chapter of Colossians, we are told that Jesus is the image of the invisible God. Similarly, I could never see my Father, nor could anyone else because he is beyond what our sensory apparatus can detect, except for audibly as reported in scripture and that I report later. But my Father, who is eternal, has allowed himself and his nature to be revealed through his prophets, saints, righteous people, and our instincts that will lead us to Jesus who is the image of my Father; just as he did before humans became separated. This, for me, means that in Jesus, and through our interaction with him, the nature of the creator of the universe and of humanity is revealed. So that Jesus, who is the tool created by the Divine, will reveal the nature and characteristics of our Father.

Our sensory apparatus speaks to us

The only way we know what is true is through our sensory apparatus. This is the same way that I knew love emotionally as a baby. Our senses do not have cognition or rationality to tell us what love is but provides our emotions with data that allow our emotions to speak more eloquently than any intellectual definition of love can speak to us. A person can say 'I love you' or 'I love your child' but only the sensory reception of emotional love can validate if a person truly loves. An infant emotionally knows their mother's love versus the one that says, 'I love your child' but is unable to love them to the extent the child knows emotionally of their love. It will be the baby's emotional response that reveals whether the person loves the child. The baby has no cognitive awareness of who the person is, but only emotionally knows the comfort and peace that come

[30]

through love. At an emotional level, we can also discriminate between masculine and feminine love, even as an infant.

My senses reveal my Father

This is what told me that the person who provided me with peace and joy in my pain loved me, even more than my mother, dad, and the nurse who cared for me. Peace is an emotional byproduct of that person's loving care and a sense of security. The three elements of security are love, peace, and joy, and from an emotional perspective is why we seek the divine who provides us with the only true peace. It is security that allows the person to trust the one who is the source of the love. These are not intellectual observations and definitions. On the contrary, it is our senses that provide our emotional system with the data that reveals to us what is real. My sensory data told me the one who provided me with peace was masculine, and over time I will identify him as my Father, the creator of the universe. Later I will say how my Father spoke to me and laid out my path. The voice of my Father changed my life, but what is important is what my senses told me was real and true. It also told me that the person at the center of my pain as a child is the same person that spoke to me nearly 40 years later. I knew this because my senses, through my emotional system, gave me peace. Not an intellectual peace but peace within my heart, a peace that provided security that is love. This book is my reflections on what my senses have told me about the divine. Therefore, it is not about any law, dogma, or ideology.

Emotional perceptions of the divine

There is only one way we know anything about the divine. This is through our sensory apparatus. We have intellectual descriptions of the divine, but these are based on the emotional experiences of a person that people attempt to intellectually elaborate on, meaning through language. The emotional encounter with the divine is beyond language and to suggest we can fully capture it is not possible. However, we do derive very useful insights via language.

The sensory data received from the environment, including our body, is automatically responded to unconsciously. For the stimuli to become conscious it must be filtered through language. In other words, regardless of the environmental stimuli our sensorium perceives, for us to be aware of it we must functionally have non-instinctual language. I am not speaking about a medical definition of consciousness that has an infant as a conscious being. I am suggesting that an infant is functionally an unconscious being in the same way all hominins whose language was instinctual are unconscious. So, for the person who had an encounter with the divine, within their emotional system they received and unconsciously understood the encounter as peace, security, and love. But to fully describe the encounter via any language is simply not possible.

For the hominin with instinctual language any emotional response of any kind will remain unconscious but will impact the hominin's emotional memory. For those who have a non-instinctual language our emotions still function at an unconscious level, but after the emotional event we can begin to reflect on the event, always in our non-instinctual language. The stronger the language the greater the reflection. The most common way our ancestors and we today encounter the divine is unconsciously through our emotions.

One further point about how we function. In modernity, and with consciousness, we have intentionality to behavior. I have the intention to go into the kitchen but once I begin the movement I don't consciously think about every step or action to get there. The intent is sufficient, and functions unconsciously. After I get there my next set of intentions become part of my behavior without having to think about each movement I make. The point is with consciousness comes intentionality and is a product of free-will. The infant, of less than a year, isn't functioning with intentionality because it has not yet developed non-instinctual language. The infant is functioning fully within its emotional system. As it learns language it also is learning about free will, and therefore intentionality. Our ancestors who had only non-instinctual language, behaviorally were driven by instincts, their emotional memory of events functionally became part of their instincts or lost. For them and us, behavioral instincts are products of emotional stimuli over millions of years and always related to survival.

Emotional awareness of the divine

The hallmark of an encounter with the divine is peace. Our ancestors encountered the divine because the divine is imbued within us. We were created to be with the divine, it's an instinct and immutable. The first contact with the divine was emotional and, therefore, unconscious. In the same way I encountered the divine in my pain of polio and know that the person I encountered was masculine but also had all the compassion and empathy of a female. However, I did not know this at the time of my encounters, but only after I developed non-instinctual language. I can never fully articulate the encounters because non-instinctual language is not capable of it. I understand this to be that the divine is for hominins all the qualities of male and female but is always perceived in the masculine.

Our ancient ancestors encountered the instinctual qualities of the divine for millions of years but in the same manner I did, emotionally and therefore unconsciously.

Eventually, humans began the arduous process of developing non-instinctual language to discover the gods, their emotional memory of millions of years of encountering the divine. Over thousands of years non-instinctual language evolved. A byproduct is, to varying degrees, based on the strength of the language, free will and intentionality. This is focused on survival and the worshipping of the gods. Just as their instincts drive them to survive, so does the instinct to be with the divine drive them to worship the gods. As I noted above, the manner of our ancestors worshiping the gods is not like we do, which is more intellectual and controlled. For our ancestors for tens of thousands of years as non-instinctual language is immerging, it was more about encountering the divine emotionally, and then attempting to reflect on the experience. Not like we can reflect but more from what we would call, awe, and emotionally desirable above all things. This will continue until we develop civilizations. Consciousness and language are strong, with free will and intentionality. We no longer reflect on the encounters of the divine as our ancient ancestors did. Humans have a more robust language that is sufficient to create oral noetic, meaning a generalized way of thinking. This is the first noetic that allowed humans to think about the divine and to see the divine outside of their emotional experiences. However, they still longed for the emotional encounters because of the intimacy with the divine.

With the literate noetic of today we still have the instinct to worship or know the divine but with the literate noetic we unconsciously interpret reality in an abstract manner, while our ancestors with an oral noetic viewed a concrete reality. This means our free will, intentionality, and noetic are somewhat different than our ancestors. In the same manner children under the age of eight view a world differently than their parents.

If we want to see the way our ancestors thought, we only need look at those less than eight years of age. Everyone will pass through the evolution of our species, from conception to about eight years of age when they develop a literate noetic of modernity within a fully phonetic alphabet. For those whose noetic is an oral noetic, they will acquire it at about age four to five.

Becoming separated

From a theological perspective, being separated from God is what we call sin. This is a very complex process that has been part of our evolution from the beginning. But we are separated from God in ways the traditional theology does not address. Separation from the divine is very different depending on the type of noetic one has. So, separation as understood and experienced by Moses, the prophets, and Jesus and his apostles is different than what we understand as being separated today. Sin therefore is different, depending on the noetic one has. There is universal sin or ways to separate from the divine that crosses all noetics, this is slavery of mind or body. It is a direct attempt to make the slave worship the slave master. This all comes about through the development of language and the byproduct of laws, dogma, and ideology.

Language, consciousness, free will and intentionality all provide humans with much more power over nature; therefore, the ability to survive is greatly increased. The oral noetic has a tremendous advantage for survival over the pre-oral noetic that our ancestors had while emerging into consciousness. An even greater advantage is achieved with a literate noetic. However, there is a downside to this power. With each stage of human development, we grew further and further away from the divine. By this I mean, further away from emotionally experiencing the divine as what we

[35]

did prior to becoming conscious. This means that via the evolution of language, consciousness, intentionality, and free will, humans were slowly separating from the divine. Humans slowly and unknowingly were sinning. Not by breaking what we understand as a commandment of God, but simply developing more and more powerful languages.

Those with an oral noetic, even today, are emotionally closer to the divine than those with a literate noetic. We all generally worship the divine but emotional contact with the divine and the sensory experience that accompanies it is impossible to achieve. We must get into what we generally call an altered state of consciousness to have a lived emotional experience of the divine as our ancestors did. There are several ways to achieve this, but generally it is through deep prayer, meditation, chanting and drumming (the use of sound), and forms of hypnosis. This is necessary with a literate noetic because of the propensity towards the abstract instead of the concrete, and thus the literate noetic naturally interprets things more towards the eternal. But even the person with an oral noetic will still have difficulty encountering the divine because of language.

For example, Jesus' prayer to his Father and his encouragement for us to pray as he does, has two different understandings depending on the persons noetic. "Our Father who is in heaven," is understood by those with an oral noetic as the divine being emotionally intimate to the person. For the person with a literate noetic the divine is in heaven, generally understood as an eternal location of the divine that we at some point in the future might enter. Two very different understandings.

The beginning of the end

The evolution of non-instinctual language is the beginning of the end for humans having an idyllic

[36]

relationship with the divine. We call this period of human history as being in paradise and is the story in Genesis. It is a story of a collective memory of the beginning of the end of our emotional intimate relationship with the divine. Our ancient ancestors slowly inculcated and expanded non-instinctual language over about 10,000 years. The stronger the language or lexicon, the more profound the separation from the divine. However, the instinctual pattern of being with the divine is strong and so they continued to worship, but now within language, as we do today.

Language, the source of separation
from the divine

For our ancestors who were developing non-instinctual language, they could still establish some elements of their lost relationship through worshipping the gods. Their natural state of their noetic was mostly functioning out of instincts, with varying degrees of intentionality. In other words, it was easier to get into what we call an altered state of consciousness. There is a collective memory of the time when humans walked and talked with the divine. This memory became part of oral tradition and when language could be written this memory was recorded in the story of the Garden of Eden. By oral tradition I mean this was part of lived experiences and our ancestors wanted to account for the reason their ancestors had an intimate relationship with the divine and why their relationship was slowly slipping away. In an oral culture where the stories of their ancestors were presented as if they were still occurring, their sense of time was unlike ours. These were oral cultures that lived in a very concrete reality without abstract thought. This process began about 25,000 years ago and continued for almost 20,000 years. These are time scales we cannot fathom. Non-instinctual language continued to grow very slowly for

[37]

nearly 20,000 years until writing was invented. The oral stories of our ancestors, and likely creation stories that were part of oral tradition would become written beginning about 6000 B.C.

So, the evolution of consciousness is a byproduct of non-instinctual language, which in turn is the reason humans are not in union with the divine as our ancestors were when they only functioned with instinctual language, language developed through several iterations. With each change came a greater lexicon that dual stochastically was the product of a wider range of experiences. All language prior to the invention of a fully phonetic language by the Greeks in about 750 BC., was what is called an oral noetic. For the past several hundred years such a way of thinking was known as Eastern Philosophy, because in modernity we recognized that the ancients did not think as we do today. There were a few differences, but in its simplest terms, stories were oral, even written were oral, and observations of the environment were concrete without any abstraction. For example, heaven is the stars and other celestial bodies, and not a place of the divine, or souls.

Western Philosophy, as it is known in modernity, is the way we think in the West. People educated in Western thought across the planet have what we call a literate noetic. This is the education of choice because of its power, particularly in the sciences. By educated people I mean those educated in a fully phonetic alphabet. I will discuss further but for now studies have shown that it is the fully phonetic alphabet that has transformed the manner that humans think. In essence, there are two types of thinking that we have as humans, at least after we become fully conscious. These are the oral noetic of our ancestors after becoming conscious and for those who have inculcated a fully phonetic alphabet their noetic is literate.

[38]

This is an example of the relationship between consciousness as a byproduct of non-instinctual language, and the manner in which the brain functions depending on the structure used by the person's language. Non-instinctual language produced an entirely different noetic than our ancestors who were still speaking an instinctual language. Slowly humans began to add the ability to write in their language, and for those who were efficient also developed a new noetic. They were both an oral noetic, meaning thinking was non-abstract and conceptually very concrete. The last noetic to evolve is the literate noetic based on a fully phonetic alphabet and dual stochastically transforms the person's noetic of being oral to a literate noetic.

Because the way we think is based on the structure of our language, every generation passes through these noetic phases outlined above, at least to the level their language affords them. In a modern Western country, a baby is born unconscious and passes through all the different types of noetics and finally at about the age of eight or nine have developed a literate noetic. So, every person potentially will pass through the entire linguistic history of humanity. They will begin in non-instinctual language and will complete their noetic odyssey with literate noetic. I propose that there is a new noetic emerging, that is not yet fully realized. This is the noetic of Artificial Intelligence.

The product of consciousness, free will

There are several byproducts evolving out of instinctual language. One is free will that begins its journey to the manner we exercise it as humans are developing a more complex instinctual language. At this stage our behavioral instinct governs most of what our ancestors do, as well as a child. As our ancestors began to open the door towards consciousness, free will became stronger. With consciousness comes an oral noetic and free will is more a product of the way the person thinks. The oral noetic's exercise of free will, as it regards the divine, is intentional. Those with an instinctual noetic worship the divine as an instinctual necessity. With the literate noetic free will is stronger towards abstract ideology. So, for the noetic of modernity, worship is far less an emotional encounter with the divine and much more intellectual with laws that govern what constitutes the way we worship and what constitutes being separated from the divine.

Traditional understanding of separation
from God is inadequate

Those who live in their head live in their vocabulary, as if words are real. This is the ground for laws, dogma, and ideology; an artificial world that is believed to be real. Such people mimic behaviors that they believe reflect their law, dogma, or ideology that they foster. Words are not real but are symbolic. We functionally behave as if words are real. For those who accept words as functionally real at some point they experience a psychological phenomenon that we call cognitive dissonance. This is a conflict between what their senses are telling us versus what words are saying and what is true. For example, the words of the constitution of the United States claim that all men are equal, and we create laws to reflect what these words mean. However, functionally we experience that all men are not equal, cognitive dissonance. Or, in scripture in the gospel of Matthew in the seventh chapter, Jesus tells us not to judge. However, religions judge others all the time. They determine the laws, then judge others to make sure individuals follow those laws. And then, we are told God is love and the experience of enforcing laws versus our experience of love do not match, again cognitive dissonance.

From the perspective of individuals and groups whose belief is similar, cognitive dissonance is the psychic energy that drives the person towards trying to solve their psychological issue between what their sensory apparatus is telling them that is true versus what law is saying to be true. This will result in conflict of one type or another between those who hold the dogmas versus those who seek change. This results in stress, guilt, and emotional annoyance towards that which is believed to be real; that is, the words or language. Those who accept such ideologies become angry at existing culture because it is resistant to new ideologies. Another example is words can be used to change beliefs. An example is how people are brainwashed. This is where words are intentionally used by others to present a dogma or ideology that is oppositional to a particular culture norm or to a given culture. This was the mechanism that started the Second World War. It is perhaps the most common way we have today for one ideology to overthrow another. I am not suggesting that all changes in culture are bad, only that this is the process that accompanies change. I do suggest, however, that attempting to enslave others, physically, or ideologically, is evil.

At times, change is necessary. However, any change must be consistent with nature, meaning our instincts. Any other form of law, dogma, or ideology that is outside of our instincts is an attempt to function outside of divine law, not good, futile, and very destructive to humanity. This results in separation from the divine. Those who buy into such ideologies are blind to Truth and become impervious to divine law. They work at undermining individuals and culture to become free to implement that ideology. First, they create the ideology, based upon a half truth, and as individuals become a slave to the ideology it becomes dogmatized. The next step is to form laws that keep all the slaves on the plantation and training them as soldiers of the ideology who are at war with those who are not on the plantation. No one on the plantation is free, nor do any of them live in any form of peace, and therefore have separated themselves from the divine.

This same process occurs with an individual, even when that individual has no desire to change culture. Instead, they attempt to change their own set of laws and dogmas that they inculcated into their own set of values and morals. This change will allow them to behave in a manner that satisfies their new ideology but at the expense of functioning within the cultural norm of their upbringing. The same emotional and psychological process will take place. They will have a sense of cognitive dissonance, guilt, anger, and most importantly a lack of peace. The human experience of peace comes to us from the divine when we are in concert with him. When we do not have peace in our life, we are outside of the divine and separated from Him. To steal, lie, commit adultery, etc. will result in the process outlined above occurring. The reason is such behaviors may provide a sense of fleeting happiness, but it never provides peace. Why? The answer is simple. Such behaviors are outside of our instincts for survival, but function within their parameters. Guilt is the component of our instincts that tells us we are outside of divine law and need to change or to repent. Also, we cannot experientially have peace in our life when we have guilt.

An example of this is a person who is unsatisfied with his financial state and begins to consider how to get more money. At some point he begins to focus on illegal ways to get money and if he does not stop that type of thinking he will begin to act on it. He has introduced a new ideology into his personhood and begins the process of acting on it. Once the act is completed, he feels guilt and if he does not change or repent, and the same ideations continue, the person will create a dogma and laws that while are internal for the person are rigid and they are now a slave to the internal law. Whether it is an individual or a social movement the processes are the same. They validate, via intellectual argumentation, that their postulated theory, although outside of our instinctual parameters of being in union with the divine, is valid. However, our senses are unable to say it is true, and therefore it is not true until validated by our senses, but people behave as if it is true which will result in guilt and anger.

A worldwide phenomenon is climate change. This is an example of what I am speaking about, but it is a more secular example. This is an intellectual theory that uses something every person on the planet is connected to for their existence, the climate. Theory suggests that the climate is changing in ways that are detrimental to humanity's existence and therefore is an existential problem that must be solved. Notice how there is an attempt to link the ideology of climate change to our senses. Every storm that has a substantial impact on cultural structure is evidence of climatic changes, and thus sensory evidence of the dogmas and laws that have become an instrumental component of cultures around the world. As the theory postulates, the planet is getting warmer and that is what creates larger and more dangerous storms.

What is the fallacy of such ideologies? It is not that the planet is getting warmer, for in fact it is and has been warming for at least the last 30,000 years, long before humans had any impact on the climate or any ideology that suggested warming is an existential threat. This is the natural warming cycle that brought an end to the last ice

[43]

age. Without global warming we would likely still be in a neolithic or post neolithic world, Also, we would still be unconscious functioning out of our instincts. Population levels would be about the same as they were 25,000 years ago, perhaps not much more than 100,000 people worldwide.

The center of wokeism and ideological theories that are fabricated in the mind without sensory verification, for the United States, is the Northeast. This area would still be at the bottom of over one mile of ice as part of the glaciation of the last ice age. Europe too, would be a frozen environment. So are those who do not want the climate to no longer change, saying they want to return to the last stable climate we had, the ice age. The earth has done very well over billions of years without some intellectual ideology assuming it knows better than Mother Nature. The natural process for the climate on this planet is to change slowly but change. Not just the climate but also land masses are in a constant state of movement. There is simply no way that we could produce enough food to support over 4 billion people with the food and resources we need in ice-age conditions. The threat to humanity is ideologies that suggest humans can control and/or change the climatic weather cycles or anything else. Humans need to care for the planet and do whatever we can to keep it as close to its natural state as possible, but not at the expense of making every person a slave to ideologies, laws, and dogmas. The most grievous way we can be separated from the divine is slavery and therefore the most diabolical. Everyone is separated from the divine because everyone is a slave to laws, dogmas, and ideologies. We don't need any more.

When I say everyone is imbued with laws, dogmas, and ideologies I say that these are the structural elements of non-instinctual language and the components of civilization.

[44]

If we are civilized, we are separated from the divine. What keeps a person in line within a culture? It is its laws that are based on a dogma that was derived from an ideology. When we explore the story in the book of Genesis about the Garden of Eden, we find two people who are in concert with the divine and at peace. But as soon as the Serpent enters the picture and the ideology: from the Serpent, you will not die, humans create the first ideology in the Hebrew scriptures. This will become dogmatized in that the fruit pleasing to the eye and desirable enter the heart of the woman. The law now says anything in the garden is good to eat. She gave the fruit to her husband, and he just followed the law because he was a slave. When the divine discovered what the humans did, he expelled them from the garden before they could eat the fruit from the Tree of Life. No human law, dogma, or ideology can be in union with the divine because slaves are unable to totally focus on the divine; for a slave will always think about their master or even masters.

This seems hopeless

This indeed is a hopeless situation if it wasn't for the desire of the divine to be in union with his people. People have recognized this dilemma from the beginning of conscious history. We have developed all manner of laws, dogmas, and ideologies to overcome the situation, because we have an instinctual necessity to be with the divine. Our earliest civilized cultures created religious laws that if followed would allow humans to come into union with the divine again, by either an actual spiritual sensory encounter or by a psychological phenomenon of psychosomatically having a spiritually induced artificial encounter. This continues today. I am not suggesting that laws, dogmas, and ideologies are the only cause for our separation from the divine. The truth is the primary reason we are separated

[45]

from the divine is consciousness and its dual stochastic companion language. However, the manner that the dual stochastic nature of language functions is typically through laws, dogmas, and ideologies. The nature of non-instinctual language is the way it configures or structures the manner we think.

There are individuals who overcome the laws that governed their response to the divine and achieve a unity before death. They are always outside of the dogmas of their environment and consequently are seen by those in authority as being a major problem to their ideology. Religions are structured out of laws, dogmas, and ideologies, and are themselves a source of separation from their desire to bring people into unity with the divine. Again, this sounds hopeless. However, religions offer people a way to get on the path toward the divine and are very helpful. But with the advent of a fully phonetic alphabet religions are themselves an obstacle because of their laws, dogmas, and ideologies. What we call faith in God is really belief in God, for faith is experiential with an emotional encounter with God that is always outside of dogma. People easily become slaves to religious law and place more energy into following the law than God. It is their personal emotional encounter with God that we instinctually desire. No new dogma or law will result in getting people off the plantation.

The connection between Truth and Scripture

The product of the fully phonetic alphabet transforms the sensory apparatus of the brain from being centered on sound as with the oral noetic, to one centered on vision that distances the person from physical reality. Hebrew scriptures are based on an oral noetic and are very close to our sensory observations of reality and reveal aspects of the characteristic of the divine that are revealed through our

[46]

senses that validate what is true. Remember, in the Acts of the Apostles, (Acts 9:1-31), the conversion of Paul via an encounter with the person of Jesus occurred via the spirit of the divine and not because of the preaching of the apostles. On the contrary Paul received authorization from the High Priest in Jerusalem to travel to Damascus to arrest and bring Christian believers back to Jerusalem for trial as heretics. In other words, Paul was living in law and using law to judge others for being outside of the law. But my Father, who is Love, allowed him to have a personal encounter with the person of Jesus, and this encounter spoke more eloquently than any preaching of the apostles, even though the apostles spoke about their personal encounters with Jesus before and after his resurrection. Paul was not judged, but God believed in him and knew that he was seeking God and believed that by enforcing law he would become closer to God. It isn't speaking about encounters with the person of Jesus that allows it to happen but the will of my Father whose desire is to be with everyone.

The Law of Love

God knows laws, dogmas, and ideologies separate us from Him, for he is the one who created us. So, religion is not evil, but its laws can become controlling and antithetical to the law of love. This is the only True Law because it does not create slaves and is always freeing. In 1 Cor. 13:4 ff: we are told that Love is patient, kind, and is not jealous, nor is it pompous, it is not inflated or proud, is not rude, it does not seek its own interests, it is not quick-tempered, it does not brood over injury, it does not rejoice over wrongdoing, but rejoices in the truth, it bears all things, believes all things, hopes in all things, endures all things. Love never fails. All these attributes are antithetical to law. Religious dogma truly attempts to function within them but unfortunately

[47]

succumbs to the easy road of creating law. Jesus says in John 8:15: I judge no one. Jesus is living within the Law of Love and is the way back to the Father.

Hebrew scripture is not about intellectual argumentation, as in the Christian New Testament. They are about the sensory experience of a people's lived encounter with the divine in the Old Testament, and about accepting Jesus as the Messiah in the New Testament. Both testaments provide us with insights into truths, as do other holy scriptures. However, the insight of humans that reveal divine love are at times difficult to understand, as in the gospel of John and Jesus saying he judges no one. This is very difficult for us to accept because we live in a world of laws and judging is part of the law. We think that without judging others we will fall into chaos, and perhaps so. But I think we are looking at the problem all wrong and need to apply it more directly to ourselves and not culture or religions. Having a modern noetic and coming into relationship with the divine is about being righteous, being at peace, and living in the joy of the Holy Spirit (Rm 4:17). If we live within the Law of Love we will also be in the Kingdom of God, on earth and if on earth we will have no issues after death.

5

The Path
(Being on or off the path)

Sin for our Hebrew Ancestors vs Modernity

To better understand sin from the lived experience of the Hebrew peoples who gave us what sin is and how we become separated from God, we must remember that their noetic was oral and much different from ours; that is, a literate noetic. For our ancestors who had an oral noetic, and specially the Hebrew, sin was functional and therefore their journey to God was in the here-and-now and understood as a path. The path is experientially based on the life of a nomadic lifestyle. Travel through the wilderness is based on landmarks and the trails or paths that are established lead to places with water. To venture off the path was detrimental for the survival of the one who gets lost. Because the path was a matter of survival, the Hebrew concept of behaviors that separate us from God is also just as important. They used this everyday experience of survival in the wilderness as the image for sin.

So, throughout the Old Testament we find the image of being on or off the path. This is a reference, or better an image, of sin. It is an image because images are based on something functional. The reason for this is their noetic was incapable of thinking in the abstract, except by concrete inferences. Sin was not an abstract idea, but always a lived experience. This means that offending God was not directly related to an afterlife as it is in modernity. The image is a journey from birth to death and that journey is functionally a path. Stay on the path and all is well, you will arrive at the path's end; venture off the path and you are lost.

This is unlike sin in modernity that is theological; meaning, intellectually based on Greek philosophy. In modernity our literate noetic naturally places sin into categories and lists them in degrees of severity. Greek philosophy is the effects of a literate noetic that is the psychic results of the invention of the fully phonetic alphabet by the Greek about 750 BC. Once the person who has an oral noetic can read in a fully phonetic alphabet, there is a transformation in the brain, specifically the way one thinks. In modernity this transformation occurs at about the age of eight years. But for now, I am saying that the reason the Hebrews had a concept of sin different than we do in modernity is two different noetics. This is exemplified in modernity with children. A child of five knows right and wrong and is completely functional; this is because they have an oral noetic just like our Hebrew ancestors. We all know that children of eight or nine have a different understanding; theirs is more abstract because their brain is transformed by the inculcation of a fully phonetic alphabet via reading.

The Greeks understood a similar idea of being on or off the path. However, their understanding was intellectual and abstract. Sin is a behavior, like the Hebrew, but the behavior that is identified is abstract. By this I mean, what comes first is the idea of a sin, while for the Hebrew it is the behavior that identifies the sin. This permits an intellectualization of sin. We can conceptualize any behavior we think can separate us from God and that becomes sin. The idea of sin is an idea, that if the idea is a behavior, then that behavior is a sin. The Hebrew oral noetic would not understand such a concept.

For example, in modernity, we have the Seven Deadly Sins as the model for what is sin. These are: pride, envy, wrath, gluttony, lust, greed and slothfulness. These are understood as severe enough to permanently separate us from God. But what are they? How can I have pride that separates me from God, especially if I take pride in my love of God, my family, neighbor, or country? Or to a lesser degree do I have pride in praying? What are the grounds that will make it prideful for me? How much prayer, or type of prayer, must I have to avoid sin, or the amount of time I pray, or not enough, the style or type of prayer? God is love and I should seek his love with my whole heart; what does that functionally mean? How do I sin within this idea? What does this functionally have to do with pride, or for that matter any of the deadly sins? At a functional level it is a bit confusing. The same can be said for each sin. This is unlike the understanding of sin for the Hebrew or anyone with an oral noetic. The specific behavior is the sin; a behavior that is close is not.

What is the path?

Below I will discuss the accepted notions of sin and note how the Hebrew understanding is functionally experienced, the product of an oral noetic. But now I will address the path. The Greek understanding, meaning the New Testament, except for the Acts of the Apostles is based in a literate noetic. The path is an abstract idea. When it speaks about sin, or having the correct relationship with God, it is in abstract phraseology. This is exotified in the description of being on the path in Galatians for a literate noetic.

[51]

14 For the whole law is fulfilled in one statement, namely, "You shall love your neighbor as yourself."

Note how quickly the whole of law is placed into discrete abstract behaviors and how we really don't know how we transgress behaviorally.

15 But if you go on biting and devouring one another, beware that you are not consumed by one another.

This is punishment for transgressing the law.

16 I say, then: live by the Spirit and you will certainly not gratify the desire of the flesh.

The Spirit is an abstract translation of the Hebrew path. To follow the Spirit is to come to God and his kingdom; that is, not on earth but in the heavens.

17 For the flesh has desires against the Spirit, and the Spirit against the flesh; these are opposed to each other, so that you may not do what you want.

18 But if you are guided by the Spirit, you are not under the law.

This is a radical change to the Hebrew idea of the path and one's journey to God. For the Hebrew the boundaries that define and identify the path is the Law. Now the literate noetic understands the path in abstract terms and calls the path, the Spirit. By Spirit they are saying that because the Spirit is God, then being within the Spirit you are not under the Law but now within the domain of the Law giver and not subject to the Law.

19 Now the works of the flesh are obvious: immorality, impurity, licentiousness,

[52]

20 idolatry, sorcery, hatreds, rivalry, jealousy, outbursts of fury, acts of selfishness, dissensions, factions,

21 occasions of envy, drinking bouts, orgies, and the like. I warn you, as I warned you before, that those who do such things will not inherit the kingdom of God.

I want to point out several things about these verses. Notice how quickly the abstract noetic classifies and categorizes what is sinful. The author states these sins are obvious; but without saying what behaviors they are nor how they are associated with sin and to what degree one must function within a category to sin. Also, each category is abstract, and anything that is abstract is very difficult to identify precisely. This is very much like the Seven Deadly Sins.

22 In contrast, the fruits of the Spirit are love, joy, peace, patience, kindness, generosity, faithfulness,

23 gentleness, self-control. Against such there is no law.

Again, we see the propensity towards categorizing and classification, but of the thing of the Spirit, and each item that the author identifies is abstract. And as with sin, we functionally know what these attributes are. This is a problem for me in writing this book because so much of it is functional but the modern noetic has difficulty in the functional, and naturally interprets something that is functional to abstract ideas. Below are verses from the fifth chapter of Galatians and is a very good description of the path but from a literate noetic.

24 Now those who belong to Christ [Jesus] have crucified their flesh with its passions and desires.

25 If we live in the Spirit, let us also follow the Spirit.

[53]

Note how the idea of Christ Jesus is now infused into the Path or Spirit. Belief or faith in Jesus means that we are infused into the Spirit and like Jesus are outside of the flesh. There is an implicit idea that living in the Spirit has in some way removed the person from the things of the flesh. But again, what does this mean? What is the flesh? Do I no longer have to eat, drink, work, keep warm, have a family, et cetera? Or do I do these things in a way that is within the Spirit that we don't understand or recognize? The Hebrew life was more of a functional journey that was to keep the Law as given by Moses.

Regardless of the noetic, to be off the path is a sin. The real issue is what constitutes the path. Is the path for our ancestors different than in modernity? To be off the path is to be in sin, and to be on the path is to be in concert with the will of God, and I would say following our instinct for the divine, which is true for the Hebrew and Christian scriptures.

The ancient Hebrew's understanding was about getting back on the path and, therefore, about the here and now, not eternity. So, if one got back on the path, they were functioning or behaving within the Law of Moses; this means the Ten Commandments. The Ten Commandments were understood as the functional boundaries of what defined the path. In modernity, and the literate noetic, to be off the path is about being eternally lost, and to get back on the path is about one's eternal salvation. My point is not that one understanding is better than the other but that they are radically different. Each has its limitations and strengths, however, we are unable to validate that something is real without sensory validation, so we need both.

Regardless of the sin, either from within an oral or literate noetic will always be functional. You cannot sin abstractly. Further, keep in mind the notion of sin in

[54]

modernity as exemplified by the Seven Deadly Sins: pride, greed, wrath, envy, lust, gluttony, and slothfulness. While we cannot see the functionality of the Seven Deadly Sins, we must ask, what are they? In other words, we do not at once recognize them as a naturally occurring behavior. This is not the case with our ancients who understood sin from the perspective of its human behaviors, and how the sins laid out below are behavioral.

All religions, past and present, have sin, meaning forbidden behaviors, as the way for the devotees to stay within the behavioral parameters set out by their god to be in his good graces, all arising out of cultural epoch from which the religion emerged. What follows is the generally accepted understanding of sin, and a more scholarly description of sin both from an oral and literate noetic. Unless otherwise stated, sources including unidentified quotes are from Strong's Concordance, Douay Rheims Bible, Ancient Hebrew Resource Center, or myself. The definition and pronunciation are provided for each word in the first citation.

So, what is the sin of wandering from the path?

Faith, in both Scripture and the writings of the Fathers, is often depicted as a journey to God. But sometimes we wander from the path of righteousness, either intentionally or not. This is suggested in the Hebrew adjective, *rasha`*, which means *wicked* or *criminal;* specifically, in the sense of departing from the right path. The word is used in this sense in Psalm 18:21, "Because I have kept the ways of the Lord; and have not done wickedly against my God." But many other translations flesh out the literal meaning with the phrase "wickedly departed." A similar idea is conveyed in the Greek verb, *plamao*, which has a basic meaning of *to cause to stray, to lead astray, lead aside from the right way*.

Note how the Hebrew is linked towards specific behaviors, while the Greek notion is linked to ideas that can be applied to behaviors. As for the Hebrew understanding, wandering off the path was viewed from the behavior to the idea and the Greek understanding is from the idea to the behavior. This will be true throughout the discussion on the idea of sin, and in modernity with our literate noetic. This is the effects of an oral noetic of the ancient Hebrew versus the literate noetic of the Greeks and the noetic of modernity.

Sin as missing the mark

Another standard Old Testament word for sin is *chatta`ath*, which simply means *sin* or *sinful*. (It also refers to the offering made to atone for that sin.) But the word has a rich origin, coming from the verb *chata`*, which among other things means to miss, miss the mark, miss the way, being off the path. In the New Testament its Greek counterpart is the verb hamartano, meaning *to miss the mark* as well as *to wander from the path* (the two noun versions are *hamartia* and, less commonly, *hamartema*). In the literal sense, *hamartano* could be used in two contexts. First, we could speak of missing the mark when you shoot an arrow and miss the target. Second, you could miss the road you were supposed to take. This reflects a common circumstance of sin: we have good intentions, we aim for virtue, but we still fail to achieve it. As St. Paul wrote in Romans 7:15, "What I do, I do not understand. For I do not do what I want, but I do what I hate (evil)." In modernity, we would never accept the idea that because I miss my turn-off on the freeway that I sinned. But this is a profane concept defining a divine reality. Being off the path is problematic for a person, especially when it comes to the divine. It is their

[56]

behavior that is the determinate as to whether they have missed the mark.

Sin as being broken

One of the most common biblical words for sin is the Hebrew word *ra`*, which has the basic meaning of *bad* or *evil*, appearing over 600 times. It comes from another verb, *ra`a*, which can mean essentially the same thing, but also refers to something *broken*, or, more specifically, broken into pieces. This helps us to see one way that something can be said to have gone "bad." A broken chair is a "bad" chair, it can no longer perform its intended function of bearing the weight of a person sitting on it. The same goes for food that has gone bad, it is no longer suitable for eating. *Ra`* is still used in this literal sense in the Old Testament. For example, in Kings 2:19 we read that the waters of Jericho had "gone bad." Truly sinners are broken people, unable to live the rich life of communion with God for which we were created.

Sin as being blemished

Ra` can also refer to a blemished animal that is unsuitable for sacrifice (for example, in Leviticus 27:10 and Deuteronomy 17:1), which offers us yet another metaphor for sin. A blemish is a mark or defect that ruins the perfection of something. Something that is blemished has been deformed in some way. Truly this is what sin has done to us. Humans are made in the image of God, but that image became deformed or blemished in the Garden of Eden. How often in scripture the person or group with skin disease, blindness, or the mute, are seen as being sinful, or the product of the sin of others; something Jesus rejects. This blemish requires repair, and it is Jesus who leads us back to the state of being unblemished as we were before the fall in

[57]

the Garden. Again, we see the sensory function of what constitutes a sin.

Sin as crookedness

Used more than 200 times in the Old Testament as a word for sin, the Hebrew noun `avon refers to *perversity, depravity, iniquity*. Its root is the verb `avah, defined as *to bend, twist, distort*, or *to make crooked*. This reinforces two metaphors for sin mentioned above: sin makes our paths to God crooked and it also distorts and twists our nature into a contortion of what we were created to be. But fundamentally, `avon are behaviors that bend, twist, or distort anything that is about our journey to the divine.

Sin as rebelling

Fundamentally, sin is a rebellion against God and His authority. This is denoted in the Hebrew noun *pesha* and its verb counterpart, *pasha*, both referring to rebellion. Put simply, rebellion is (usually violent) resistance to some authority. Normally this is what we think of as the first sin: resistance to the highest source of authority possible, meaning God. Below I will offer an alternative view of the first sin from an instinctual point of view. But *pasha* has a subtle element of violence in the story, implied in the 'eating' of the apple. *Pesha'* is constant with how the woke, and elite foster the demands of social pressure on individuals who do not comply with their ideologies.

Sin as trespassing

Appearing about 30 times in the Old Testament, `asham is a verb that refers to sin in the sense of offending, being guilty, and trespassing. A similar New Testament Greek word is parabaino which can be defined as to go by the side of and to go past or pass over without touching a

[58]

thing -- or, more specifically, to overstep, neglect, violate, transgress (the related noun is parabasis). This is a metaphor for sin instantly recognizable to anyone who has ever said the Our Father: Forgive us our trespasses, as we forgive those who have trespassed against us. Adam and Eve tasted the 'forbidden fruit,' a form of trespassing or `asham'. The Greek understanding is much more general in that these are ideas that can be applied to many things that are not sinful, while the Hebrew is about behavior and more specifically how our psychology responds to behaviors that cause guilt or shame.

Sin as debt

It's worth noting that the actual Greek words in the two gospel versions of the Our Father do not literally mean trespassing. The one in Matthew is the ancient Greek word for debts, opheilema. (It's used only one other time in the New Testament, in Romans 4:4, in a similar context.) In the version of the prayer in Luke, a form of this word for debts and *hamartia* is used, so literally the verse would read: Forgive us our *sins* as we forgive everyone *indebted* to us.

Sin as desolation

One secondary definition of 'asham' refers to the ultimate consequences of sin: utter desolation. This is how it's used in Isaiah 24 in haunting imagery: "See! The Lord is about to empty the earth and lay it waste; he will twist its surface and scatter its inhabitants. Therefore, a curse devours the earth, and its inhabitants pay for their guilt," or, as some translations put it, the inhabitants *are desolate* (New American Bible, Rev. Ed.). Again, we see the psychological impact of behaviors that separate us from the divine, and then described with words that are about the effects of sin.

[59]

Sin as drunken swerving

When we wander off the path, we often are not in our right minds. This is conveyed by two Hebrew verbs that have almost identical meanings in *Strong's Concordance, ta`ah* and *shagah*. Both can be defined as *to err, to go astray*. Digging deeper, the additional meanings tell us something about the corresponding state of mind: *Shagah* can be defined as *to swerve, meander, reel, roll, be intoxicated, err in drunkenness*. Likewise, *ta`ah* can mean *to be made to wander about, be made to swagger like a drunkard*. In Proverbs 5:20, *shagah* is also used to describe a young man's physical "intoxication" with a prostitute. Keep this idea of intoxication in mind when you read "stray" in this petition of Psalm 119:10, "With my whole heart have I sought after thee: let me not stray from thy commandments."

Sin as oppressive toils

One New Testament word for evil or bad is the adjective *poneros*, which literally means full of labor, annoyances, hardships, or pressed and harassed by labors. I am reminded of the slavery of the Hebrews in Egypt as sin and how God freed the people from the burden of sin. Surely sin is an oppressive toil that for us, as humanity, could never be complete on its own. I also suggest that laws, dogmas, and ideologies at their heart are *poneros*, and will oppress the people by its weight of control. In Matthew 23:4 Jesus rebukes the leaders of Judaism that lay heavy burdens, laws, on the people that they themselves do not follow, a form of slavery, while the yoke of Jesus is light and without institutional law. What makes them light, from my perspective, is to follow our instincts to the divine, but with the guidance of religious authority because of their experience and study of God.

Sin as impiety

Another word for sin in the New Testament is *asebeia*, a classic ancient Greek term for impiety, which referred to a lack of reverence and respect for the gods. For the Greeks, the attitude of piety implied distance from the gods; yet for us, our relationship is a much closer one. God is not some sky spirit who hurls down thunderbolts from Olympus; instead, he is as close to us as imaginably possible. He became man and invites us to share in His being through the Word, sacraments, and our relationship with others. Nonetheless, it is still healthy to maintain a holy fear of God, something affirmed in the Bible. As Proverbs 9:10 says, "The fear of the Lord is the beginning of wisdom."

Sin as lawlessness

Aside from the laws that govern any society, there is the natural law that is written on the hearts of all men, as St. Paul said. Hence, some wrongdoing may not be against the law of a particular society, but it still crosses God's laws. A modern example is abortion. Regardless, whether it is legal or not, it crosses the law of God, thou shall not kill. In this context, it makes sense that the New Testament writers also spoke of sin in terms *anomos*, the Greek antonym for *nomos*. This was one of the most important words in ancient Greece. It did not mean only the law, but the law in the sense of rules and established norms of behavior that have been established through custom and tradition. Surely this is a fitting description of the law revealed to the Israelites, which had been handed down over the centuries and remained a decisive force in the spirituality of Jews in the time of Jesus. *Nomos*, then, reflects the fact that God works

[61]

MY WALK WITH MY FATHER AND JESUS

in history and over time to teach His people how to follow His precepts. One of the biggest issues in modernity is *nomos* and is the way evil attempts to destroy the past to prohibit people from having any grounding to their life.

Sin as injustice

Another key word that is related is *dike*, the ancient Greek word for justice. Its antonym, *adikos*, is used to describe unrighteous and unjust people of the Bible. Whereas anomos, or lawlessness, highlights the offending act, adikos, draws attention to the person who commits it: an unjust person is one who breaks the law.

Sin as intrinsic evil

While sin is often described in terms of its consequences for us and others, it's important to remember that sin is an intrinsic evil. This is conveyed in the Greek word *kakos*, an adjective which simply refers to something of a bad nature or something that is base, wrong, and wicked.

Sin as bound to punishment

It's also important to remember that sin not only has consequences, a broken humanity, a fallen world, a disordered creation; it also makes one liable for punishment. This idea is conveyed through the New Testament Greek word *enochos*, defined as bound, under obligation, subject to, liable. According to Strong's Concordance, it can be used in a technical sense, "denoting the connection of a person either with his crime, or with the penalty or trial, or with that against whom or which he has offended." This is the sense in which Jesus uses the word in Matthew 5:21-22, "You have heard that it was said to them of old: Thou shalt not kill. And whosoever shall kill shall be in danger of the judgment. But I say to you, that whosoever is angry with his brother, shall be in danger of the judgment."

I conclude from this and from encounters with Jesus there is an instinctual and immediate judgment incurred on all sin, because it is the judgment that is intended to bring about reconciliation. This divine judgment is not a punishment as much as a way of attracting the attention of a person that is out of sync with the divine and needs to repent. I have found that when people are sick generally it is *enochos* at work in them, to be healed via reconciliation.

We see from the above descriptions of sin that it has a rich, complex, and behavioral set of meanings. However, from my perspective sin is about being off the path, regardless of how, why, or when we go off the path. I say this because any sin separates us from the divine and thus off the path.

Applications in modernity

In medieval times the Christian Church began the process of codifying sin and developed a more abstract version and concise list of sins; namely, the Seven Deadly Sins. All sin is deadly because regardless of the sin one is separated from the divine, and because we are not in union with the divine, we are living in sin. Most sins in modernity are predicated on deceit by the art of misdirection, the same deceitful behavior as the Serpent in the Garden of Eden. The claim is postulated as an existential threat to existence, but the truth behind the threat is fabricated in such a way as to allow people to think that the threat is something that only those establishing the threat can solve, a self-proclaimed savior. Well-meaning people are seduced by these progressive ideologies, become devotees and promulgate these ideas as a slave without recognizing their complicity to evil. People who buy into the ideology become enslaved in the same way the Hebrews did in Egypt. No slave is free to seek the divine, for the freer a person is, the richer and deeper they are free to find and walk the path. This is why Satan, as the personification of Evil, always attempts to enslave people.

Examples of sin in modernity can be found in the way people attempt to implement sin into their interactions with others. These are people whose focus is to intentionally defraud, embezzle, for the purpose of things of value that will provide them with security, generally money, but also can be power that will accomplish the same thing for them. Outside of physically forcing people to give up their possessions, the primary way people try to become powerful is through law, dogma, and ideology. These three principals have thousands of years of being practiced but it's in modernity that it has reached its pinnacle.

Introduction to laws, dogmas, and ideologies

I will be referring to laws, dogmas, and ideologies throughout this book and I want to define what I mean by these terms and how I understand them as interacting with the human condition. While it seems that I am prejudiced towards laws, dogmas, and ideologies, I want to point out that, from my perspective, they are a two-edged sword. Without laws, dogmas, and ideologies there would be no civilizations and humans would be living as we did for millions of years on the African savannahs and in the trees.

However, the very thing that brings us civilization also is the very thing that can keep us slaves to modern cultures. We instinctually seek the divine, and as part of our instinctual search, we can inappropriately worship aspects of a law, dogma, or ideology. So, whatever we consider divine, or all-powerful, will be worshipped. This is the issue with

[64]

laws, dogmas, and ideologies, as those who ascribe to them can falsely worship them by becoming a devotee, gathering others to their beliefs in what they reverence as a truth and how one will be saved by becoming a devotee. When the divine is replaced by law, dogma, or ideology, the devotee becomes a slave to what they worship. Examples of this are fascism, communism, neo-Marxist, climate alarmist, and even political parties. They all can become the source of enslavement that make them evil because these intellectual creations can keep people from seeking God; that requires freedom and is why we are endowed with free will as part of human instincts.

Difference between religious dogma and civil dogma

What then is the difference between religions and dogmas that are functionally the same? In my opinion the primary difference is that civil dogmas postulate their truths without the divine being part of their structure. Religious dogmas have the divine as their primary structure. However, religious doctrines always run the risk of enslaving the devotees in the manner they postulate their doctrine.

They tend to avoid questions, such as, was any person saved before the institution of their dogma? What about their commandments held by the religions to honor and love mother and father? If at some time a person wasn't saved, for any reason, you cannot honor them because it was the divine that condemned them, and you can't go against the divine. So, if the divine has condemned them we are not, according to religious dogma, to love them anymore. There are several such questions that religious doctrines avoid because, from their point of view, it gives the devotee too much freedom. Am I against religious doctrines? Not in any way, as they are critically essential for the survival of

[65]

humanity. But I suggest that at some time in the future they overcome the fears of their loss of power. Remember that where fear exists, the divine is not present.

Even though their use of power is benevolent, it's still about making the devotee restricted in some way. In the gospel of Mark 9:38-41, those who are not against us are with us. According to the word of Jesus and other prophets, those who work to bring others to the divine are all that is important, whether the person follows a particular religious dogma or not. In other words, it is the divine that is the most important and not a religious dogma that believes it is the only way that the divine can be found. Protestants and Islam, as well as other religious dogmas, hold to a very similar notion and should be open to their own position to bring all peoples onto the path to the divine.

All these examples have one thing in common: they foster a human need that they will solve, thus becoming a type of savior. In fact, at their core is a falsehood, and those who provide leadership will lie to keep the law, dogma, or ideology alive, but because only truth will survive in the world such figments of intellectual creations will always come to an untimely and generally a destructive end. The divine is not, nor can it be, contained within any law, dogma, or ideology. The creator of the universe cannot even be contained by the universe itself. Also, God is love, and laws, dogmas, and ideologies are by their nature antithetical to love. So, while civilization can reveal the glory of our creator, humans slowly reveal the mysteries of the universe, and we can also become a slave to that which we need.

What do I mean by law, dogma, and ideology?

First, is law. A law is a rule or set of rules that regulates behaviors or actions that are implemented to control or enforce what the law relates to, with penalties for those who violate the law. I don't want to discuss if a law or laws in general are good, bad, or somewhere in between. Instead, I am concerned about the psychological effect on a person and how the effects of a law can restrict, dampen, or just close what I call paranormal human attributes and the search for the divine. Culture directly and indirectly imposes law on culture and such laws at their heart are about controlling behaviors and actions. It is the issue of direct or implicit control of behavior that shapes the way a person will think, and it is the way that we think that creates barriers to what we recognize as paranormal attributes, and especially a lived encounter with the person of Jesus. If a person believes that he or she cannot do something for fear of punishment, such attributes will not occur, nor the instinctual search for the divine. The question a person should be concerned about is what cultural, societal, familial, and educational laws we unconditionally accept without ever thinking about them. If one takes a few minutes to reflect on how many laws there are that control aspects of their life, I believe they will be overwhelmed by the number.

The next way we are controlled is by dogmas. Dogmas are very dangerous as they are postulated as always and completely true, and that is what makes them dangerous. Dogma can also impose law, meaning punishment, when the one who accepts the dogma does not comply with the tenets of the dogma. Dogmas are generally found in religions, philosophic argument, political systems, components of culture, scientific principles, educational systems, and even every person's philosophy of life. Like law, to violate a dogma is to incur the wrath of devotees of the violated dogma.

The problem with dogma is its implicit understanding as being truth and, therefore, carries with it much more emotional energy than law because humans place the most significant aspect of their existence predicated on dogma. This is true across time and culture because it is directly related to our existence and continued existence after death. If you belong to a religion, a political party, or believe in a scientific system, or that one's family is elite, poor, middle class, educated, or uneducated, etc., you are imbued in dogma. The problem is while these observations might be true, with a small "t," they are not entirely true as they can all change. As with law, we are inundated with dogma, everything from the Constitution of the United States to our religions and why our family is different from every other family. All of these will and do have a controlling factor in the way we think, and it is the way we think that is how we behave and the attributes we have or don't have. It is the way we think that is the biggest obstacle to having a personal and lived encounter with Jesus. In other words, our prayer life is defined by the way we think, and the way we think is defined by the laws, dogmas, and ideologies that we have as part of our mindset.

The last of these characteristics are instrumental in the manner that we think. Ideologies, theories, ideas, or paragons are achieved through acceptance of an intellectual construct that may or may not be true or even possible. Again, like dogmas, ideologies are supposed to be true, and, like a dogma, truth is fundamental to what we understand and accept as what is real. The problem is that ideologies and dogmas and even laws are all intellectual and outside of sensory perception, that may or may not be true, and generally is only partially true. Ideologies are 100% intellectually generated and always with an agenda to achieve an outcome that is postulated by the ideology and outside of our senses.

Things like values or cultural mores, ideologies are always found in laws and dogmas. Like laws and dogmas, the world, particularly in politics, is full of ideologies, social organizations, fraternal groups, religions, and the like are ideological in nature and are generally the source of most of the world's ideologies. In all cases ideologies are about changing specific people or organizations to a new set of behaviors that reflect the postulated ideology. The world has its growth and evolution based upon ideologies. By its very definition, ideologies are about transforming the way a person thinks, and it is the way we think that allows for compliance to family, culture, and national norms. Because these norms are about controlling people, only those who, for whatever reason, are somewhat rebellious will ever have some form of paranormal attributes. One's life is controlled by cultural ideologies and to resist them is very difficult. Think of how many different ideologies you have encountered during your life and ask why they no longer have merit.

I am not saying that all laws, dogmas, and ideologies are bad but without such mindsets being tested and validated by one or more of our five senses, we can find ourselves enslaved to them, and then our life is focused on that which enslaved us. God is not about the enslavement of his people because without the ability to exercise your free will, you will not seek God, or if you do, God is not primary in your life, but only that which enslaved you. So, how we think, and what we think, is the foundation of how we see the world. The ideology that claims you cannot see the divine while you live, will, by its tenets, be a stumbling block to prayer that seeks the face of the person of Jesus. Very sad!

Overcoming laws, dogmas, and ideologies

The following scripture verses offered to the people by Jesus are about overcoming laws, dogmas, and ideologies. "Unless you change and become like a little child, you cannot enter the kingdom of heaven." (Matthew 18:3) A child has about as clean a mental slate as possible. Jesus is saying that the child is closer to Truth than those who have married laws, dogmas, and ideologies. Remember Jesus is telling this to men who are well versed in Judaism. A child's life is fundamentally dependent on what their senses reveal, rather than the intellectual elegance of some law, dogma, or ideology. Laws, dogmas, and ideologies are outside our senses. How many civilizations have come and gone over the past 15,000 years? And regardless of the civilization, it is always founded on an ideology that was backed up by dogmas to validate the ideology and then enforced by law. A child knows none of that and I believe this is what Jesus is speaking of in Matthew 18:3. And, from the perspective of our senses, heaven is not in some ethereal plane that humans can only enter until death and that one must live a life that follows laws, dogmas, and ideologies that are in vogue during the time that they were alive. Instead, the child is participating in the kingdom of heaven when he or she experiences the righteousness of others, and peace, and joy that come only from the Holy Spirit, paraphrased from Romans 14:17.

"Blessed are the poor in spirit, for theirs is the kingdom of heaven." (Matthew 5:3) Like a child, the person who has a poor spirit, I believe, is an adult whose life is simple, tied to their senses, and one not filled with an abundance of laws, dogmas, or ideologies. The more educated the person is the more likely that via their education they will look upon such people that Jesus calls the "the poor in spirit" as being simple minded, ignorant, superstitious, et cetera, but these are people who have resisted the dogmas and ideologies of others, and have, to the best of their circumstances, maintained a mindset free from laws. They trust what is real, which is revealed to them via their senses, instead of manmade and artificial realities.

"Blessed are the clean of heart, for they shall see God. Matthew 5:8." Again, this verse is an example of a person whose heart is clean, meaning free of being enslaved to the laws, dogmas, and ideologies that surround them. They become a little child who trusts what their senses tell them and not what their senses are unable to validate when they experience the effects of some law, dogma, or ideology. Ask yourself why it is that people living in major cities are more likely to be those who are enslaved to a governmental ideology, while those who live outside of major cities seem to be much freer and resist what is being postulated by governmental bureaucrats as being good for them. Such people live closer to the senses, and they see those bureaucratic ideologies, and those fostered by intellectual university professors, where they live primarily in their heads and very far from their senses, are not truly interested in their instincts. I suggest that when Jesus calls the "clean of heart" are those who kept ideologies outside of being controlled by them. The intellectually elite can have no greater honor bestowed on themselves than having their ideological theory become dogmatized and turned into laws. For them, this will validate that their ideology is valid because it is now a law, with no regard to what their senses tell them about their ideology. Such people do not have a clean heart, as it is full of things that are not real and are extremely far from being able to see God in this world and

[71]

will have their work cut out for them in the next reality. It is very difficult to overcome sin, and by like manner it is very difficult to overcome laws, dogmas, and ideologies, at least sufficiently to have a personal encounter with the divine.

6

MY PATH
(The beginning of my path)

From what I just discussed about sin, laws, dogmas, and ideologies, I must point out that I am just as imbued with them in my life as all other people, with some minor exceptions. What I have encountered has given me a view of the world that most do not have. I am blessed with diseases, injuries, surgeries, the way my parents raised me, and near-death experiences, that along with my occupation and education afforded me a rather unique life. I also have a very strong personality and one that can be a little overpowering for some. I also experience the same laws, dogmas, and ideologies that everyone encounters, however, I have always been rather skeptical of them. In retrospect, I understand why my Father allowed me to live a life where the circumstances of my life awakened spiritual attributes that permitted me to interact with emotionally wounded people, and those who were sick and dying in such a way as to allow the Holy Spirit and Jesus, at times, to heal their malady. These spiritual attributes or gifts taught me to work at overcoming the hardships in my own life and to trust in His providential guidance, and so, my soul is at peace. The person whose influence and guidance that allowed me to know my Father, at least to the degree I have achieved, is

Jesus. I didn't personally meet Jesus until I was thirty-seven years old, although I instinctually knew him in my early teens. I do not believe in God or in Jesus. No, I know them in the same way I know anybody, through a physical encounter.

It was at this point in my journey that sin became important to me, not just in terms of eternal salvation, which is important, but in terms of having a personal encounter with the person of Jesus. Sin made it difficult to achieve an encounter with Jesus. At the forefront of such an encounter was sin and the necessity for reconciliation. Jesus always is about redeeming the person who is lost, or off the path. He is about recreating or restoring the damage done by the punishment of guilt brought about by sin. At the heart of sin, from my perspective, is laws, dogmas, and ideologies of modernity that deceive people into accepting things that do not exist. As I noted above, sin is always bound to punishment, in my opinion, at the unconscious hands of the sinner. I see this punishment as being self-inflicted, as an unconscious way to atone for their sin, and therefore an instinct.

An example is my sister, who I love dearly, and as I pointed out above lived with my aunt and uncle for the first ten years of her life because of the depression. This experience left an emotional scar that 80 years later brought an end to a beautiful person after fighting cancer for almost ten years. The scar was a judgment of her mother that she just could not reconcile. True for many people. But my Father is eternal, as is his love. As we all sin, we are all off the path, but the path is eternal. The word eternal means: lasting forever, without beginning or end. So, death is not a barrier for humanity who are all on the path, even if they do not know it. In the fullness of love is eternal life.

Meeting Jesus

There is an emotional, psychological, and physical difference between knowing about someone and physically interacting with the person, and the more important and critical the meeting, the deeper and more profound the relationship. This is the case for anyone who meets my Father or His Son, born of a virgin over two millennia ago. Jesus is the Father's visible love to all who meet him. This book is not about me but about my Father, His great and miraculous love for His people, and how He demonstrates His love through the providential power of the Holy Spirit and in the person of Jesus. If lost, or off the path, Jesus is ready to guide you back onto the path. His actions are about overcoming sin and getting you as close as he can to the Father. The person seeking the Lord must remember that the obstacles that are preventing an encounter with the person of Jesus are the laws, dogmas, and ideologies culturally imbued into the mind that govern the way they think. Overcoming such sin is accomplished when the person is ready to forgive the person who grieved them, so the person of Jesus can experientially forgive. Unfortunately, my sister was not ready to completely forgive. It is forgiveness of others that opens the door to Jesus and dampens our cultural mindset. This will be seen in several encounters with the person of Jesus in Episodes 6-8. I cannot overstate the importance of sin, its need to be reconciled, and Jesus' healing hand. It doesn't make a difference what the sin is, whether those laid out above that are held by the Hebrews or the Seven Deadly Sins or sin from other religious groups. In my opinion, anything that separates us from one another in any way is separating us from the divine because the divine is imbued within every person. Sin is functionally identified within the person via their instincts. It is our instincts that allow us to know how we are separated from the divine and it is Jesus who heals our soul. "Do unto others as you would have them do unto you. Matthew 7:12."

Getting off the path

For me paranormal gifts or attributes are normal as being part of our instincts and therefore natural, although many have difficulty with exercising them because of their mindset. All these different attributes, in my mind, seem to be the reason why I am different, but everyone is unique and therefore different. When I became an adult, I did what I thought the world was asking me to do. But the only thing that happened was, I made a mess of whatever I did. The world was asking me to follow the things of the world and not to seek my Father. But with great consternation and emotional turmoil, that lasted about three years. I left the world and decided to serve my Father, not having a clue what that meant. After I decided to serve my Father, another several years passed before I knew what I was to do. I don't mean I knew where or what I was going to do, but the vehicle I was going to ride. That was to become a deacon in the Roman Catholic Church. I suffered greatly with that decision because of laws, dogmas, and ideologies, that I could see were prevalent in the Church.

It was important for me and for anyone to declare who they were publicly. Not for some ego trip, but to publicly declare who you are. Life is grounded in social activities and relationships, the first is family then community. Being alone is a life of despair, loneliness, and isolation. I live with Jesus, the Holy Spirit, and my Father; I am never alone. My family and all my ancestors are always with me. I live in peace, joy and being able to see some truth. I am not happy and never have a desire to be happy, as happiness is fleeting, and a person will always tire of that which makes them

[76]

happy; while peace and joy are unending, and one cannot become bored with being at peace. Happiness is a worldly allusion that is the Serpent's attempt to lure people off the path. Any allusion is a sin and will need repentance.

EPISODE 3
Aptitudes and how they came about

7

The Foundation of my Beliefs

My aptitudes

Earlier I spoke about the evolutionary trek of our species. This is a complex story that demonstrates a divine being at the heart of our journey. I suggest that part of our evolutionary instincts is what we call paranormal psychic aptitudes. These are things like pre-cognition, leaving one's physical body and travelling to other locations, seeing the energy field around a person, moving objects, knowing something by intuition that was unknown (like when some will die), physical healing, being able to suddenly speak an unknown language, and at least a dozen other paranormal abilities. These abilities are not experienced by most and those who do experience them might discount them as their imagination. Some, however, experience one or more of these abilities at times or at will. Such gifts may last a lifetime, perhaps only once, but generally they begin early in life and slowly become more and more difficult the older one gets. This is because as we age, we inculcate laws, dogmas, and ideologies that are detrimental to such attributes. These are attributes that our species have demonstrated across history and are associated with the spiritual component of humans, and, as we all know, not experienced often by most.

It is from the perspective of my understanding of how I came to have, what most call, paranormal abilities that is the topic of this episode. There are many people who have more spiritual gifts than I do, and I don't think of myself as special in any way just because I have some gifts. I believe all people are endowed with paranormal attributes, but they are unaware of them because of the number of laws, dogmas, and ideologies that are inculcated into their identity. One of the characteristics of paranormal gifts is how sin affects them. Generally, sin dampens or even stops paranormal gifts. At other times the person may, at an unconscious level, attach themselves to an evil spirit, meaning a non-corporal being that has aligned itself with Satan's opposition to God. Generally, this occurs because of some unreconciled judgment made at some point in time. In such cases we may see the person that we identify as being possessed demonstrating all manner of paranormal abilities. This is what we see in the movie The Exorcist.

Overview of my attributes

Any of my behaviors that might be considered paranormal are normal because they are part of human instincts, but not seen very often. These abilities range from mentally communicating over long distances with animals, people, and spirits of an unknown identity, and with the dead, to other types of attributes like bending spoons and moving small objects. Some types of electronic devices can function abnormally, especially computers. Writing this book is a real challenge because the computer constantly initiates commands that I don't want or request; it is very frustrating. There are other attributes like streetlights turning off as I passed under them, and then come back on after I passed them, even watches stop or might run backwards. Most attributes seem to have a mind of their own, as they function outside of my conscious will, but at times I could initiate an attribute.

[82]

Many of these behaviors or attributes were noticed by people outside of my family and I was referred to Rhine Institute of Parapsychology at Duke University when I was 12 years of age. I was accepted to be studied but my parents would not allow me to go.

I used the gift to help others when I could, like airmen in training to help them memorize their studies via hypnotism, or a person with a deep-seated emotional problem, or fear. This gift would reappear when I would pray with people, not in the form of hypnotism but the use of its general techniques for the person to come into the presence of the person of Jesus.

I also seem to have some type of affinity with death and could see when a person was going to die within about three months. Somehow, I could see death on a person's face and at first, I was emotionally troubled and wanted to help them, but I never succeeded. If I saw death on their face, they were going to die, and I couldn't change it; this is something I still don't understand, and it leaves me very perplexed as to why I have the gift but unable to do anything about it. I can only pray for them and be open to any overture on their part to talk about their situation. However, most people had no idea they were going to die, and I never felt I should say anything to them, at least directly. As a hospital chaplain, I knew when many patients would die. At times I knew exactly when they would die many hours before they did. I knew exactly when my dad, mother, and sister died from miles away, and when my wife died, I was about half a mile away and she came to me and kissed me goodbye.

The effects of having gifts
Coupled with my childhood relations with others, the social relationships I had in school, even through college, in

[83]

my business life, and as a deacon, I was treated as if my existence was to be avoided unless they needed something. I always thought I lacked social skills because I was introverted and labeled as anti-social in high school, but I eventually came to understand the issue was that I have a particular gift that makes people very uncomfortable. That gift is seeing a person's soul, allowing me to know the stain of sin, not a specific sin but the generalized condition of the soul. Almost all people live a life that is shielded by their self-created persona that is designed to make others like, trust, and accept them. But if someone can see through such a façade and the person knows or feels that you know them because you can see past the façade, they are unnerved. No one likes that someone can see them as they are; the primary reason people are fearful of God who they see more as a judge than as love. This response by others towards me, I believe, is unconscious, and people just feel uncomfortable around me. Those who get past the fear of me seeing who they are, find me fascinating and like that I can provide them with much about who they are and/or how the world impacts them. They find this very interesting and helpful in their life journey but never allow me to become part of their life within a social context.

After living most of my life, I can only come up with two possibilities as to why I have such abilities. The first is that God directly intervened to give gifts, which I am very uncomfortable with because it suggests that I am different and have something others do not, and if God gives special gifts, it flies in the face of free will that one receives the gift without knowing it. The other reason is that through instincts, a combination of my innate personality, sicknesses, injuries, and the way my parents gave me freedom and did not overly try to lovingly inculcate dogmas, laws, or ideologies while I was growing up. All these things

[84]

serendipitously opened my mind to what I call gifts, or attributes. As I got older, the education of the world and how it indoctrinates became part of my mindset and weakened my gifts, so that over time I had a hard time doing many of the things I once could do. Once a person becomes indoctrinated, it is extremely difficult to overcome the indoctrination. It leaves a scar on the person's mind and spirit, and until completely purged, it will keep the heart of a person unclean or impure.

The cost of having aptitudes

I think of myself as having paid a heavy social cost for my aptitudes, as I lived a life of being much more alone than most, of knowing my Father and being blessed by spiritual and psychological gifts, but all of this separated me from others. It also is my accounting of how my interaction with others, and using my spiritual gifts, have shaped who I am; and central to that is, what I believe, or, what constitutes what is real for me. Over time I have attempted to account for the paranormal human abilities that I possess but have no real answer although I speculate why I have such abilities. My life is one without normal social interaction with others as I seem to make people uneasy when I am around them, including my family. From my perspective, I am okay with that as I am very uncomfortable with being in the limelight, and when some paranormal event occurred with a person, I tried to make sure I was not the focal point.

I am very independent, virtually raising myself without direct parental involvement. This never made sense to me because in the early portion of my life I had a history of being sickly and my parents were very attentive in caring for my diseases, but outside of that allowed me to care for myself. When I was four years old, I entered kindergarten. My mother enrolled me but on the first day of school I

[85]

walked to school and entered by myself. I didn't understand why all the kids had their mother with them and why so many were crying "when mom left." My mother and dad worked, and my sister was in high school, so I was left to myself. I learned to cook by the time I was ten years old, would travel across the city of about 100,000 using the bus system, anywhere I wanted to go, which I tended to do. For example, I would go to the theater on Saturdays and spend many hours there watching cartoons and movies. Such a trip was at least 15 miles one way, requiring two bus transfers to get there, which, for a seven-year-old, was unusual. I generally played in the yard, but I spent a lot of time in the mountains as our back yard was the base of the San Gabriel Mountains. No one knew where I was, but I would come home before dark. I had one friend who I met when I was four and two other friends when I was ten. We are still friends, but outside of them they are the only friends I had during my childhood.

My sister married when I was eight years old and after the wedding everybody went to the reception. I was not informed as to its location. I looked for my parents after the wedding and after all the pictures were taken but couldn't find them; I was at the church by myself as everyone went to the reception. After about an hour I was still there and was ready to get on the bus to go back home when a friend of the family came to see if I was there because they asked my parents where I was as they hadn't seen me at the reception. No one knew where I was, so they decided to see if I was at the church. I was grateful to see them and to go to the reception, but I was not concerned as I knew I could take the bus home if I was left at the church. I was asked if I was concerned or hurt that nobody thought enough to make sure I went to the reception; my response was no.

When I was 11 years old my dad and my brother-in-law's dad were moving my sister and her husband's possessions to their new home about 40 miles from where we lived. About eight miles from our destination someone ran a red light and hit our truck broadside. My dad and my brother-in-law's dad were taken to the hospital, as were those in the other vehicle. The truck was towed, and I was left there by myself for about four hours until someone in my family came to get me. I don't know how my family knew I was there, nor was I concerned that I was left there. The police left without saying anything to me and I wasn't sure how I was going to get home, but I thought it was okay, as I could find my way home, although it would take time. I was concerned about those who were injured but they seemed to be okay before going to the hospital. I decided to wait, hoping my sister would miss me and find out where the accident took place and would come get me. I finally got home and was asked by some people that were there supporting my mother if I feared being left alone. My response was no. This event seemed to be normal.

Another example: I woke up on a Saturday morning to see that my mother and dad were taking their luggage out to the car. On the table was a note telling me they were going on vacation. They left me a note because they didn't think I would be awake before they left. They told me they would be back in two weeks. My sister moved and bought a house about three miles away, so she was available if I needed something; I was 12 years old. The strange thing about this example is that I thought it was normal and I was unconcerned about them leaving. In thinking about this event and other similar events, my parents must have known I could take care of myself, which is positive testimony about how I was raised. However, I believe I had very loving and concerned parents, who, if I gave them a grade

[87]

on parenting, they would receive an "A," but must say, in retrospect, I was very challenging for any parent.

So, my early life was built around being alone, but I really wasn't alone as I was filled with a sense of peace and joy that I discovered because of being sick at an early age, and it was my sickness, especially polio, that grounded me in the divine who I would eventually call my Father. Therefore, central to who I am and what constitutes reality for me is based a great deal on disease and injuries and being very independent without having a need to be with others although I enjoy the company of people. They just don't seem to be thrilled to be around me, at least socially; so, I give them what they want by not being personally needy and give them their distance from me.

I know thousands of people but while we greet one another in passing, they are not interested in socially spending time with me. I was approached one day by a member of the medical staff where I worked. Out of the blue, she said, "Do you know why the staff doesn't associate with you?" I said, "No." But while I didn't say it, I really didn't care why. She said, "People are afraid of you because everyone thinks you can see their soul and all their sins and faults." My response was, "You are correct, I can; but I don't judge you or anyone." She summed up the way people in general, except for a few, deal with me. Her comment was very helpful for me.

I believe my parents were not interested in passing on to me any emotional issues they personally had because I was still recovering from polio and, from my perspective, might have tried to protect me from social interaction with others, since polio carried with it a strong social stigma. Culturally, we were still coming out of the depression and entering the Second World War, and my sister had just come back to live with our parents. This left a severe emotional

[88]

scar on my sister that nobody knew about until many years later. So, my parents had a lot on their plate, and I greatly admire them for not passing those issues on to me. Other than life, this was their great gift to me, not passing laws, dogmas, and ideologies on to me. This also is something, I pray, that my wife and I did for our children as well, but only they can answer this question.

8

Paranormal Attributes
Where do these Paranormal Human
Attributes come from?

I believe and suggest that everything that a human can do is contained within the human instincts; we cannot act, behave, or function outside of human instincts, and further, our instincts were given to the species millions and millions of years ago. It contained the blueprint of what eventually becomes us, including what we call paranormal gifts; generally attributed as a gift from the divine. The divine in our creation provided such abilities within our instincts. Any gift or functional characteristic that is rarely seen is still part of the normal repertoire of human behavior. If a person does not have the ability to manifest such a behavior, it isn't that they are not chosen by the divine to display such a gift or ability, but that there are mental blocks to it being manifested because of the interiorizing of dogma, law, or ideology blocking them from being able to behaviorally demonstrate it. From my point of view this is related to their free will and how they chose to believe in and orient their life. Such things, by their psychological nature, create emotional fears that will prevent the behavior. When it comes to creativity, fears are deadly. This is why children are creative when they are young, and it disappears as they grow older.

This means as far back as we want to follow the evolution of humanity, such gifts were present because our instincts were part of our humanity. Also, during our paleolithic period we see paranormal behaviors routinely via the interaction between humans and the gods. Modernity's scientific evaluation of our ancestors during this period consider their behaviors revolving around the interaction with the gods as being a people who are uneducated, unsophisticated, superstitious, lacking in language that could describe their environment, and were just ruled by those whose interaction with the gods gave them power over the people, meaning priests and their religious dogmas. The truth is, while some of modernity's observations have merit, a better description of our paleolithic ancestors is a people who had a very clean heart and their actions with the gods were validated via their instincts and senses.

I also believe that words are nothing more than a shadow that have no substance but merely an outline or framework of what is real; particularly with the modern literate noetic as opposed to the more ancient oral noetic. This is why I will be focusing this book on what we experience as the only true source of what we can validate as true and, therefore, we must have a sensory encounter with the person of Jesus, and just not an intellectual belief in him. I can believe anything, but simply because I believe it does not make it real. If our sensory apparatus is not fully engaged, we cannot validate that something is real but if our sense tells us it is real, that's what we believe is true and behave in accord with what we consider true.

9

Early Sicknesses
(Sickness/Injuries/Hospitalizations)

I eventually recovered from polio and was able to walk, first with a brace on my right leg and then without it. I worked very hard at restoring my body, and doing what I could, so as not to be seen by others as being handicapped; a characteristic I still have, that I attribute to just being very stubborn. By the time I was 16, I appeared to be in good shape; at least from all outward appearances I was physically normal.

At age 14 I had malignant melanoma in five locations on my back; the largest spot was the size of half a dollar. They were removed and I have not had a recurrence of melanoma. However, when I was seventy, I was diagnosed with prostate cancer and after surgery I was treated with female hormones and for about ten years it was in remission but now the cancer has recurred, so I am again receiving hormonal therapy. In all my sicknesses or injuries, I never got excited or concerned and was emotionally the same before I knew I was told I was sick or injured. I attribute this to my relationship with my Father. I would get more emotionally concerned if I knew I was going to receive an award or something of the sort; it is being a public figure that concerns me the most.

Shortly after entering the Air Force at 17, I developed Post Polio Syndrome. Now that I am in my 80's I can still walk for short distances, stand for almost two minutes, but always with a significant amount of pain. I have always had varying degrees and amounts of physical therapy and now must have hours of therapy daily, generally with heat, ice, and massage. When I go out of the house it is always with ice on the "small of my back" that helps to alleviate the pain allowing me to stand but with significant pain. The pain locks up my muscles in my back and legs and they stop working until the pain abates. I spend time discussing my polio because it is what defines me, physically and spiritually, and the way I came to know my Father. If someone came up with a cure for Post Polio Syndrome, I likely would refuse to receive it because having a relationship with my Father is more important to me.

Polio is very painful and when I was very young and recovering, everything I did revolved around pain and therapy, but most of all on my own I learned to mentally go into what I called, "my place of peace." In this place pain didn't exist and the stress of pain would leave me. So, my life is defined by polio and my ability to go into my place of peace to escape the pain; at times, however, it is very difficult to achieve. It is in my place of peace that I met the Divine and He was always present as I worked to recover. Pain was also the vehicle that seemed to open the door for my Father to communicate with me. One of the more significant times that He communicated with me was to inform me that I had a severe heart problem with symptoms the same as Post Polio Syndrome. Seven years later I had my aortic heart valve replaced which was first detected about three years after bypass surgery as part of my routine

[93]

follow up. It was monitored and when it was necessary for the surgery, again I was at peace because my Father's hand was part of the entire process. I was in the hospital for less than 24 hours which includes the time necessary to check-in to the hospital.

Wounded

As I noted above, I joined the Air Force at age 17 and was wounded. After an unsuccessful experimental surgery, I was medically discharged after spending nine months in the hospital, but I was required to report to the Veterans Administration (VA) Hospital in Long Beach, CA. The VA immediately scheduled surgery to remove my leg from just below my right hip because my leg was dead, and I would not know if I was bleeding or injured. I refused this surgery, and it took four and a half years for my leg to heal itself, for which I am very grateful. I did not allow others to dictate to me what I would have to do, at least without me evaluating what my senses told me. This is an aspect of not allowing ideology to control my life. I also learned to trust my Father as he was very gracious to me with polio, COPD, being allergic to coal dust and pollutants, and melanoma.

EPISODE 4
The Serpent in the World

10

The Garden of Eden

Portrait of instinctual view of Eden

From my perspective the Serpent in the Garden of Eden and how, from an instinctual point of view, was the story of a collective remembrance of the time people lived within their instincts and there was no sin, and the people communed with the gods. Before the introduction of the Serpent, Adam and Eve, the names given to represent humanity, walked, and talked with God, meaning the gods but because this is written from a Hebrew perspective it is God with whom they walked and talked. I also suggest that reference to talking with the divine is also synonymous with what we call prayer. This again is a collective remembrance of a time of worshiping the gods and still living with instinctual language, behaviors, and no sin, regardless of the behavior; they lived as being one with nature and whatever nature situationally demanded, the people would respond as required to fulfill the instinct for survival.

"The Tree of Life" is what happened when humans became conscious beings; they consciously now knew life and death. Animals are unaware of death as a conscious function of their thoughts. Animals are aware of death and avoid anything that would kill them via their instincts for survival, but conceptually is not personified as an end of their existence. Humans lived in the same manner, but after becoming conscious beings, death was now being personified as something personal. Prior to becoming conscious, humans began to revere their ancestors by their burial to prevent being scavenged by predators, that would become known as the desiccation of the body. So, the "Tree of Life" reflects the desire to not die as their collective memory and lived experience revealed to them, which is related to the innate fear of going into the unknown and is the source for continuing our instinct for survival by living eternally, and thus overcoming death.

The "Tree of Good and Evil" is a functional remembrance of how, after becoming conscious beings, we discovered that certain behaviors were detrimental to relationships, and survival was highly dependent on having good relationships. But more importantly, we pined for the relationship we had with the gods, where we talked and walked with the gods. Behaviors that promoted the best survival techniques were seen as good and those that broke the relationships were evil, the effects of bad behaviors that didn't promote survival. This is true today. This component of what constitutes good, and evil was in the making for millions of years, with things like being on guard at night to keep watch for predators while the family slept. No intrusion of a predator was good, and the intrusion of a predator without alerting everyone was evil. When humans were waking up from the sleep of being unconscious beings, there was the collective and instinctual remembrance of good and evil, and because of its importance to our survival it became represented in Eden as the "Tree of Good and Evil."

The serpent and evil

The collective memory of good and evil became represented by a serpent who was the most difficult of all predators to detect, especially at night. Some serpents were benign to humans while others, deadly. Serpents are deceptive, cunning, willing to lie and wait for their meal for hours, even days. In Genesis the serpent is the most cunning of all creatures and unlike humans and other animals is cold-blooded and, therefore, seen as non-animalistic or non-human. Our instincts also view evil as not being part of humanity because in every case where we experience evil it is against our instinct to survive, even in modernity. To be labeled as being evil allows others to assault, victimize, and justly kill because evil is about our demise. Think of wars, politics and laws, dogmas, and ideologies, and how we identify those we don't agree with as being evil.

The dialogue between the serpent and the woman in Genesis is about deceptive speech without directly lying. This is characteristic of the behaviors of a snake. They can give the impression of being benign but then strike without warning, very much like sin. We think we are doing the right thing but then without warning relationships are broken. The serpent made no overt attempt to lie, but also didn't tell the whole truth that allowed Adam and Eve, humanity, to eat the forbidden fruit. We eat this fruit daily, if not among others, for certain we gorge ourselves with laws, dogmas, and ideologies that shape our thoughts and behaviors. If you think you are not part of this story, try to go to a quiet place and concentrate on something good; for example, how you love your parents or children. How long can you do it? Most people take less than a minute. But if you do the same thing about someone with whom you don't get along, you have no difficulty in focusing on your dislike of them and how they hurt you. Evil is about leading you to a lifetime of walking off the path, and unable to pray, except perhaps discursively, meaning praying by memory or reading prayers, or praying for the demise of those you have judged as evil, easiest of all prayers.

Evil: How did it come into the world?

I notice that when I look at people, I have this overpowering sense of their relationship with God; the same is true for institutions. At first it made me uncomfortable but as I began to identify with this maxim, do not judge least you be judged, in like manner. I could also see that my task was not to judge or condemn but to unconditionally forgive and love them, even within their evilness. My time with Jesus in visions with others has taught me that Jesus loves despite our sin. In no way does he condone sin but loves the person and Jesus works with the person to overcome sin and become reconciled to eliminate the obstacle between the person and himself, to get the person back on the path.

In recognizing sin in a person or a law, dogma, or ideology, I am filled with sorrow and compassion because they are separated from the divine. What I mean by separation is that they believe they are right in their judgment, but they are blind to what they are doing. These are obstacles to love and if you can't see your sin, you will live with it until the self-induced punishment either brings you to reconciliation or kills the person. I have witnessed the way Jesus interacts with people and how, when struggling to forgive, they will see the person they need to forgive through the eyes of Jesus and then try to emulate his behavior and attitude, which is to be compassionate, love them, and forgive them. Only then does authentic forgiveness follow. I truly struggle with accomplishing these goals in my own life, but I try to repent when I fail to see the person as Jesus sees them.

[100]

One of the things I have witnessed while in prayer is that some people are terrified of Jesus because of sin. I think their terror is the result of an instinctual and deep-seated fear of sin itself as sin is, from an instinctual point of view, detrimental to survival and the way sin came into the world. Also, there is an instinctual judgment placed on sin and we are fearful of such judgment and shy away from the one who we think judges. Sin is a product of behaviors that did not promote survival of our ancestors that were evolving over millions of years, and it broke our relationship with those we depended on for survival. When one of our ancestors failed to behave in a manner that kept the family safe, it was not good, and this would eventually come to be a sin. The last thing a person wants to do is acknowledge they failed to keep their family safe from a predator because they fell asleep while on watch through the night, and the predator carried off a family member. Emotionally, that is bad for the survival of the family. Many other behaviors would also be seen as bad, like becoming lost, failing to find resources, eating food that made someone sick or killed them, and many other behaviors that are important to survival. Judgment would be might out by the family and until reconciliation took place, the person would be shunned and if the situation was unreconcilable, the person would be banished from the family, which was a death sentence.

In modernity when faced with the divine, the person who is being judged emotionally is unable to escape. The fear of being judged can be more than the person can endure and the fight or flight mechanism for their survival is activated, and the person will hide, run, or put up psychological barriers to keep them from being judged. Very sad, because they are closing the door on what they want more than anything, love. They are likely to create an artificial reality in which they live; a reality that says they

[101]

have a wonderful or good relationship with their family, or God, to think all is well. I submit that almost everyone does this and is a major reason why they cannot achieve a lived encounter with Jesus in prayer.

The instinctual fall from the path
(the Kingdom of God)

Instinctually speaking, the exile from the garden is about the permanent effect that evil has on our lives and the way it leads us off the path. Jesus calls the path the kingdom of God, and rightly so, for our ancestors Adam and Eve, were in the kingdom of God before the introduction of evil. When we are on the path, we are living truth and witnessing truth to others. But when we are off the path, we live in darkness because we are unable to see the light, which is truth. One of the characteristics of being off the path in modernity is how those who seek the divine are led to believe that they are unable, in this life, to encounter the divine, and for Christians that would be Jesus. An example of this is found in Matthew 18:20 "For where two or three are gathered in my name, there am I in the midst of them." Ask a child what this means, they will tell you that if two or more people come together to be with Jesus he will be there, not in spirit or in some theological hyperbole, they expect the person of Jesus to be there. However, we are taught that this verse is more about trusting that our prayers to Jesus will be answered because Jesus hears our prayers that rise in spirit and he who is in spirit will receive them and answer them. To me when someone is off the path and teaching others to be just like them, they are making disciples of people who will live in fear, perhaps with belief but fearful of being with the person of Jesus.

In the next verse, Peter asked the Lord, "Lord, if my brother sins against me, how often must I forgive him? As many as seven times?" Jesus answered, "I say to you, not seven times but seventy-seven times," an infinite amount of mercy for that is what our Father gives us, His infinite mercy to allow us on the path or back into the garden. We are barred from the garden because God has placed two angels with flaming swords to keep us out for fear we contaminate the garden with our laws, dogmas, or ideologies. Also, note that there is a direct relationship between forgiveness and having an encounter with the divine.

My experience with encountering the person of Jesus is not some kind of loving experience like we think of as love-ins where everything is kumbaya that was part of the last quarter of the 20th century. No, what my experience tells me is that when we encounter Jesus, and many times even before we do, we are confronted with some component of evil within our heart, generally in the form of anger and hatred. We have failed to forgive, and the wounds caused by others and unfortunately in some cases, especially in families, wounds that sometimes are institutionalized and repeated. There are scars left on people because of cultural strife and wars, and many hardships. We don't seem to forgive unconditionally an infinite number of times. We are very far off the path, but Jesus wants us to get back on the path. Such encounters with the divine have always allowed for forgiveness of others, so we are forgiven in a like manner. One encounter may not be enough to get fully onto the path, but it is a start towards returning to Eden.

We don't recognize evil and, therefore, are unable to forgive others and to seek forgiveness for our sins from others and the divine. How sad it is that people are affected by laws, dogmas, and ideologies, and then teach them to be accepted by others by making them disciples, unwittingly and functionally agents of evil.

[103]

Two types of anger

Anger is an instinct and if it is exercised in the manner it is designed, we do not incur sin or guilt. If, however, we are angry and incur sin, we are in trouble. How do we know the difference? I was always told that if I was angry, it was a sin and was a form of virtual murder, unless my anger was a holy or righteous anger. A holy or righteous anger is to be angry with anything that opposes God. Any other form of anger is very bad, like killing someone in your heart. In the Gospel of Mathew Jesus tells us whoever is angry with his brother will be liable to judgment, and whoever says to his brother, Raqa, will be answerable to the Sanhedrin, and whoever says, you fool, will be liable to fiery Gehenna. This is scary stuff because everyone becomes angry. So, if I am angry, I am liable to judgment. If I call my brother, one who follows the Torah, "a raqa," Jewish word meaning without knowing the Torah, I will have to answer to the Jewish authority, the Sanhedrin; and, if you call someone a fool, like raqa, meaning misunderstanding or interpretation of the Torah, it is because the person who is a fool is empty headed about the Jewish Law.

While Jesus was referring to Jewish Law, I think we can safely say that any anger that is associated with a passion that lasts longer than the event causing the anger is problematic for us and is a sin that takes us off the path. By passion I mean the other type of anger, an instinctual anger that is about our survival and is not a sin if we incur it. For millions of years our ancestors lived in a world that required them to be very watchful of their environs and any predators that might be a threat to them. When we are attacked by a predator we fight back, and we are angry so that our brain supplies the necessary adrenaline that prepares the body for

[104]

the flight or fight response to a threat. Under normal or natural circumstances when the event is over, we return rather quickly to our normal state. We would have a remembrance of the event and use it as a marker to be watchful when similar circumstances are observed.

If, however, we incur a threat, but we don't return to a normal state when the threat is over, we have likely attached our passions to it and we don't get over it as we should. In such a case we fall under the judgments about which Jesus speaks but from within our own cultural systems, meaning laws, dogmas, or ideologies, or most likely from within our own body, emotional, or spirit. For example, if I am out for a walk and I am assaulted, the flight or fight response is triggered and if I now judge other people as if they will do the same thing to me, I have judged them out of unrepentant anger. This is not good as it will affect us in the form of spiritual, psychological, or physical punishment even though we are unaware of it, and it is many years later. I refer to the anger my sister experienced when she felt she was abandoned. Even at a very young age the flight or fight response was triggered but she was, through no fault of her own, unable to be reconciled with the feeling so she unconsciously passed judgment on her mother and lived her life in anger with her mother. Unfortunately, it also caused sickness and eventually her death. It is my experience that for most people their physical, emotional, and spiritual problems are the result of unresolved anger. Our angers need to be presented to Jesus in whatever way we can and not just confess anger with our lips, but also forgive those who we believe wronged us. You will see this acting out in many of the situations or encounters with Jesus that I discuss in Episodes 6-8.

The world and its serpent-like behaviors

The world of laws, dogmas, and ideologies is about creating a mindset that controls people to a specific way of thinking that when inculcated into a person's mind will control the manner they think and is consequential in their behavior. This trinity of mindsets is about creating a reality that is consistent with their artificially created laws, dogmas, and ideologies. Such thinking and the development of their view of what constitutes what is real makes it extremely difficult for anyone who has accepted them to break free from their own warped view of the way they see and interact with the world in which they live. Such a world is always based on a lie and the lie is enforced by additional falsehoods, so eventually there is no truth left in them or their ideology. Failure to submit to the falsehood either as an individual, community, or culturally are pressured or psychologically coerced or physically threatened by force to obtain the results their ideology or dogma dictates. Those with such desires in their heart must destroy all that is contradictory to their evil ideology. They become so infatuated with their dogma that in their mind and heart there is no guilt, even though they are very destructive. For them these deaths are of the enemy and, therefore, they see them as non-human and deserving of being driven out of making a living, culturally being ostracized by a very few loud threatening voices, creating fear of being physically harmed, and even being killed, all for the sake of their evil and destructive desire to instill their ideology on others. They spend their time waking and sleeping, plotting the destruction of anything that stands in their way of total dominance. This requires them to attack the family unit as seen with worldwide abortion and abortive techniques, and attacks on children via education or human sexual

[106]

orientation. Then, God's people and their belief in Him, the culture itself must be destroyed to make way for a new reality where their ideology is dogmatized by force. The overall goal of any ideological lie is enslavement of the people. This evil can only be overcome with my Father's Love.

Evil will always lie and tell people the things that seemingly are good and beneficial but those who are perpetuating the lie never fulfill their promises nor tell you the complete truth. To create a fertile ground to plant the seeds of their ideology they will speak about becoming free from oppression or some outside threat and, therefore, it becomes necessary for others to accept their way out of such pending doom that they are always clothed in initiating our instinct for survival. Therefore, their lie is always about some kind of made-up existential threat to our existence. Once a foothold is established, those who foster the lie will work at attacking any institution or person or ideas that are close to or operate within the sphere of love because of its proximity to God's Love which is antithetical to their ideology because God's Love is foreshadowed with the lived experience of earthly love, forgiveness, charity, and freedom. We need to look no further than Communism in China, Russia, North Korea, and Cuba and other modern tyrannies like Nazi Germany, Fascist Italy, and many other governments in Asia, South America, and Africa. Such laws, dogmas, and ideologies are not limited to governmental power, but also with those who claim the world is ending if we do not stop using fossil fuels.

We also see such mindsets of evil in the workplace, educational environments, and social media. All such attempts to control and make slaves of people eventually are destroyed because at the heart of such ideologies is the desire to separate people from their creator and is grounded in evil instead of love. Their destruction is energized by the instinct to seek, worship, and come to God. To use Mother Nature, that has been functioning for many billions of years and has survived climate disasters far greater than anything we are facing with a warming climate, is to use evil in the most diabolical way possible. Care for our house is always important and we should do all we can, but to do so in such a manner as climate alarmists are attempting to do will result in the destruction of many innocent people.

I noted above that this book is about my spiritual life and relationship with my Father, a relationship that is steeped in confronting and destroying evil to set those affected by evil free so they might come to accept the Love of my Father and experience the person of Jesus. In this book I want to share how I am called to overcome evil with Love and Truth, and to foster a style of prayer that encourages a personal encounter with Jesus. The example above is about cultural evil, but evil is anything that keeps one from being free to come to my Father and His Love. This includes the imprisonment or being captive to false ideologies, and trying to prevent people from having an internal longing and desire for the Truth of my Father that can be found in His Word, to help those who have strayed from the path of perfection, to give those who are sick my Father's Love that they might be healed and have their life restored, to help people become compassionate, and not judgmental, and without fear. In short, we must open the door to my Father's Love that we might live as He created us to live. Jesus said, "I have come that they may have life, and may have it more abundantly, John 10." The obstacle to these beatitudes above is evil. Jesus' encounters with those I have prayed with have started the slow process of becoming reconciled with their sins and stepping back on the path.

My weaknesses and failures to walk the path

I would be remiss if I didn't address my own weaknesses, failures, and shortcomings. What I outlined above sounds like I am a saint or a person with great spiritual gifts and power; I am nothing more than a person like everyone else. At times I have experienced what I would call miracles or at least events that are out of the ordinary and they have always happened when I cooperated with the will of my Father. When I attempted to do the same thing that had brought about a healing of body, mind, or spirit, or tried to separate a person from an evil entity, I was not successful because, I think, it was about me. However, when I listened to the Holy Spirit, whatever I encountered, God's will was accomplished. It is my weaknesses and failures to walk the path laid out for me that keeps me from listening to the Holy Spirit.

Living in the world, a world that is separated from my Father, is a great challenge. Of great importance to my failures to be a servant for my Father is my personality. I am blessed with a strongly stubborn and introverted personality that has provided me with a strong will allowing me to overcome the physical effects of polio, being wounded in the military, Post Polio Syndrome, surgeries, and I am still able to walk, although I struggle to walk now. The same personality that allows me to do these things is also the source of my weaknesses and failures. As a strong introvert, I have never wanted to be in the public's eye; so, I did whatever I could to avoid publicizing my spiritual experiences, and I only revealed some of them to my wife, family, and at times a few others, so it is my prayer that my family and children come to know me better through my confession laid out in this book, and that it helps to deepen their relationship with my Father.

[109]

What I mean by being in the eye of the public is my personal, and what I consider private, spiritual experiences. I have been in the public eye for fifty years, but it is as a deacon in the Roman Catholic Church and an educator. As a strong introvert, I don't want to reveal my spiritual gifts, except privately when I am responding to the will of my Father. In my public life I could hide behind intellectualism and not reveal my true spiritual nature. It is the sum of my weaknesses that I deeply regret not making the Love of my Father known to as many people as I could have, but I was afraid of public exposure in the event of demands, expectations and being judged if I was unable to fulfill what was being asked of me. I put myself above God for fear of the laws, dogmas, and ideologies to which I was exposed.

So, it is with great trepidation that I will be laying out in this digest my spiritual experiences. But it is my belief this is what my Father wants me to do. After years of refusing to reveal my relationship with my Father, I have relented; He always wins. My stubbornness is linked directly to my will and that means I fight with God over things I think He wants me to do and at times He wins and at times I just become very stubborn and will not do what He wants. Now I pray to make things right with him.

Getting on the path in a world of evil

I will be using my spiritual experiences and then elaborate on them with either their meaning for me, or someone else, or how it impacted and/or changed my life. I will not be disclosing all my spiritual events but those that I believe have value in helping others to the Love of my Father. I will be encouraging people to pray and specifically to pray in a manner that will foster the opportunity to experience the person of Jesus; to touch His hand, feel the warmth of His body, and what He might say to you. I will demonstrate this through spiritual experiences with others and my visions and locutions, meaning the utterance of my Father.

I fully expect there will be those who will be very skeptical of what I say, but I also pray that at some point they will become open to God's love, and to look at the laws, dogmas, and ideologies in which they are imbued, and accept the freedom of God's love for them and confess their judgments that will open the door for the divine to enter. His only desire is to be with His people as we once were.

All of us, without exception, hunger for love, acceptance, and the forgiveness of sin, even when we don't believe we have sinned. We are instinctually hardwired to love and to be loved. It is sin that separates us from others and love between people and with God. So many people are blind to sin and live their life as though all is right between themselves, others, and God. Many give themselves to ideologies or people whose only interest in them is to control and fulfill their own emotional needs, or to fulfill the instinct for love by giving themselves to an ideology but only to discover they are nothing other than a slave to the ideology. Others might give themselves to laws or dogmas that seemingly are designed to bring them to God, but instead the dogmas or laws stand between them and God because the dogma or law becomes so important that it becomes greater than God and they become a slave to the dogmas, and then try to enslave others to falsely engender and become a slave just as they are. There are some who have invested so much of themselves into either a law, dogma, or ideology that to become free is the most fearful thing they will face in their life, not even death will rise to the fear they have of breaking free of the enslavement of their mindset. Some, like me, give way to their weaknesses and shortcomings that are incapsulated in their innate

[111]

personalities, which they never allow to grow and become strengthened and come in service to others, first to family, then to neighbor, to community, and lastly to see their relationship to others as their relationship to God.

[This episode is about how I believe my Father gently, yet persistently, was asking me to be a servant to Him. What follows are events that either were very earthly that I eventually took to be a spiritual encounter or were, from my point of view, outside normal human experiences.]

EPISODE 5
THE VOICE

11

My Walk without Food

In 1970 I went to Mass on Ash Wednesday, which is a Holy Day for Roman Catholics. While in line to receive Holy Communion, I seemed to sense God telling me to fast, which didn't make sense to me because Ash Wednesday is a day of fasting and I was fasting that day. The next day, Thursday, I went to Mass again and because it was early in the morning I was not going to eat until after Mass. Again, as I was in line to receive Holy Communion, I had this overpowering feeling that God wanted me to fast. After Mass, without stopping to get something to eat, I went on to work and the feeling (sense of fasting or "with a steeped awareness to fast") kept coming into my sense of awareness. At lunch time I abstained from eating. When I got home, I told my wife I didn't want to have dinner as I wanted to fast.

The next day was Friday and a day of fasting during Lent so, again I abstained from eating, but did have black coffee, and a diet Pepsi. My wife and I went to Mass on Saturday evening, and the same thing occurred; God was asking me to fast. So, I continued the fast, consuming only black coffee throughout the day and a diet Pepsi once a day. Now I had the feeling my Father wanted me to continue to fast to show him my love. He also asked me to walk to work once a week and pray while I was walking. To me, this seemed to be a bit too much as I had two offices and to walk to them both and home is 30 miles. I didn't understand and so throughout Sunday I prayed, asking what He wanted me to do. On Monday morning I decided to go to Mass and during Mass it seemed to me that my Father was asking me to walk to work every Tuesday until Easter and go to Mass every day except on Tuesdays. But the biggest request was to continue to fast until Easter Sunday. So, I was asked to go without any calorie intake for the 46 days from Ash Wednesday to Easter Sunday, and to walk 30 miles on Tuesdays. I didn't think much about it, meaning what the physical, psychological, and spiritual consequences were for such a feat. I just set out to do it. It was about a month before my wife realized I was not eating, and when I told her about it, she responded by saying, "I will pray for you."

Every Tuesday I started out for work. I had no idea what I was to be praying for as my Father didn't tell me, and I didn't ask. So, this was my prayer. Every step I took I said, "This step is for God." So, for six weeks of Lent, I walked my 30 miles and made about 52,800 steps each Tuesday repeating with each step, "This step is for God." This phrase was said about 316,000 times, Mass every day except Tuesdays, and 0 calorie intake for 46 days. I really didn't think it was so special and only my wife knew I was fasting. I still haven't spoken about it as it was just a normal activity, and nothing very special. For me, this was my response to my Father's request to show him how much I love him. After many years of reflection on my life and through the process of writing this book, I have come to believe that this event was part of my vision I had with Jesus on a lake who asked me to "Feed my sheep" and my letter from my Father 11 years later; both events are reported below.

My acceptance of my Father's desire for me
to dedicate my life to Him

At age 14, I had an experience of the divine that many years later I related to be like Abraham's call by God to follow him to a new and different world, which Abraham did without understanding where he was going, or who it was that was calling him to leave his homeland. I understood His call as God asking Abraham to dedicate his life to following God. I never thought of myself as a type of Abraham, but I was struck with the nature and manner of how I was called and the similarity to how God called Abraham. I noted above my experience on December 24th, when me and two friends were hitchhiking home after some Christmas shopping and I accepted Jesus as my savior, and I dedicated my life to God. At times I had difficulties, but I remembered my decision to dedicate my life to God and it always seemed to get me back on track.

At age 28, I began to contemplate the meaning of this event and contemplating whether to join the Catholic Church. First, it seemed to me that Jesus was asking me to join the Church; and, secondly, I knew my wife would like to see me in the pew next to her and able to receive communion. I was very resistant but eventually relented. Our instincts are about power over nature, which gives us the best way to survive. The ultimate instinct for power over nature is the divine and the instinct of the divine is within each person. The divine is always attempting to commune with each person by getting past those obstacles we place as a barrier that must be overcome via repentance. I suggest that all barriers are, at their core, "feeling sorry for ourselves." By this I mean, whenever we place ourselves at the center of our existence, we do so by making ourselves greater than the creator of the universe. This completely isolates us from those we love and especially God. So, for

[117]

me, "feeling sorry for myself" is a great sin; very much like the sin of Satan who "felt sorry for himself" that he was not God. I know that I am "feeling sorry for myself" when I am the subject and object of my thoughts about something or especially someone else.

12

Meeting Jesus on the lake

In April 1978 I was ordained as a deacon in the Roman Catholic Church by Archbishop James Casey during the reign of Pope Paul the VI. Pope Paul died in August 1978, and as part of my daily Morning Prayer routine, of two to three hours per day, I asked the Holy Spirit to guide the Cardinals in the selection and election of a new pope. About three weeks later Pope John Paul I was elected. He died about one month into his papacy. Again, I prayed to the Holy Spirit for His guidance until Pope John Paul II became pope in October 1978.

In early October 1978, while in prayer, Jesus came to me in a vision. In the vision I found myself at a retreat house where I regularly visited. On this occasion I found myself sitting on the stairs at the north entrance, a vision for which I didn't ask. As I looked down the sidewalk, Jesus was walking towards me. I was shocked and amazed! Jesus motioned for me to join him. I walked toward him until I was at his side; nothing was said. The path led us over the top of a small hill and then the path went down the hill to a lake. We walked in silence until we arrived at the water's edge where there was a small rowboat.

Looking at the lake I had the impression that this was Galilee, the lake of Jesus' ministry. We arrived at the boat and Jesus got in and then motioned for me to join him. Jesus began to row out onto the lake, still in silence, staying within several hundred yards of the shore. After being on the lake for a period, I could see thousands of people with their hands outstretched above their heads and crying out to God for his mercy. We were close enough to shore for the people to hear me, so I began to shout, "Jesus is over here! You're looking in the wrong direction!" I kept shouting and shouting but it was as if they could not hear or see me. I turned to Jesus and said, "Your people are calling for you, Lord."

Jesus got up and began to walk on the water toward the shore and I thought he was going to his people to answer their prayers. He motioned for me to come with him. I got out of the boat and walked on the water with Him toward the shoreline. My focus was on the people, and I didn't see that Jesus returned to the boat. When I realized that Jesus was no longer standing next to me, I began to panic. I called out to Jesus for help; I was slowly sinking. I was shocked that Jesus did not help his people, and it looked like he was not going to help me either. I continued to call for His help, but Jesus continued to row further onto the lake. I felt just like the people on the shore who were calling for his mercy and getting no answer. Before I sank into the water, Jesus said, "*Feed my sheep*." The vision came to an end, and I was back at home, shocked and perplexed as to what had just happened.

What did I learn from this vision? I spent years reflecting on the vision and praying for insights into what Jesus was revealing and asking of me. I learned a great deal, but I was only sure about one thing -- I was blessed with a vision of Jesus. It seemed to me there was more to be gained from the vision than its symbolism. Now I was praying for clarification of the vision, and it wasn't until three years

[120]

later and several hours of daily prayer before I got further details about how I was to "feed his sheep." Even with this additional information I am still reflecting on and receiving insights into the meaning of the symbolism of this vision. What I have gleaned thus far is discussed below.

The *retreat house* was the place I went to on retreats for years to fast and pray asking for Jesus to lead me to the Father and I believe the retreat house is symbolic of my desire for Jesus. So, for me, Jesus coming in a vision was his response to my prayers that occurred over years. The retreat house always reminded me of the Galilean hills where Jesus fed the 5,000 and witnessed the word of God to the people seeking God during the first century. We walked on a *path* to a lake, which for me symbolized my journey to Jesus and to my Father. I always viewed the stories of Jesus in the bible from the perspective of its culture, language, and environment. It seemed that the vision was consistent to my view of the place where the ministry of Jesus took place and therefore, for me, was holy ground.

The *lake* that I identified as Galilee was the place Jesus was teaching the people about the Kingdom of God. It also was the place where Jesus walked on water, and he called Peter to walk on the water with Him. My experience on the water was like that of Peter. These are symbols of faith; a faith that seems to be differing between those on the shore and my own. No one on the shore had a faith sufficient to fully connect with Jesus. I also came to realize that every miracle Jesus performed was done by one of the prophets before him, save turning water into wine, and the miracle of the resurrection, although Moses turned the Nile into blood. This realization would be important to me later in my ministry, as I recognized that the ministry of Jesus is continued by others.

The **boat**, for me, is how I am to be carried by Jesus on my journey to the Father; and when I say to the Father I mean in the here and now. It is Jesus who knows where we are going and how we will get there. My part in the journey is to trust and have faith in Him, like when I got in the boat in the vision -- Jesus provided the power, and the direction of the boat. I am to trust and have faith that he knows where we are going. Following Jesus is not easy because the world hates him and if we do follow him, we too will be hated. This is a ministry of faith in Jesus, and I will never know where I am going or how I will get there, only Jesus knows. The **ores** are the Word of God that powers my journey and will bring his people into his physical presence or the physical person of Jesus. Seeing, touching, and hearing Jesus, as in the vision, is instrumental in my encounters I have had throughout my ministry. The word of Jesus and the Old Testament is Truth and Life; that is God's Word. My task is to know His word and trust in His Word. It isn't an intellectual understanding of his Word but the mindset of Jesus and to live life as much as I can in accord with his Word that powers me through the waters of life.

I see the **people in the valley** with their hands held above their heads in prayer pleading for Jesus to answer their prayers as people of faith but are trapped by popular cultural and religious beliefs, or laws, dogmas, and ideologies that I speak about in this book. These beliefs seem to say that we come to Jesus by accepting him as our savior, just as the evangelist did in 1954 who asked me and my two friends to accept Jesus as our personal savior. If we do, we will meet him in the "hereafter," heaven. While this is true, the people were looking for more, and I think they were looking to have a personal and intimate relationship with Jesus in the here and now. Not a relationship that is intellectually grounded in our theological and historical

[122]

knowledge of scripture and about Jesus, but an experiential relationship within our heart.

For me, their **outstretched hands** symbolized discursive prayer reading or repeating words from memory particularly from a literate noetic, and impersonal knowledge, bereaved of a personal encounter with Jesus. This is intellectual and linguistically dependent knowledge and prayer in which those on the shore were indoctrinated but were still empty. It seemed to me that their outstretched hands were asking Jesus to enter their heart, but they just didn't know how to open the door, and Jesus will not go against our will. Discursive prayer also is prayer of the modern world, meaning rational and controlled. It has great value but the gateway to the heart is not rational and cannot be controlled.

The **valley** that the people are in seems to symbolize being trapped by cultural linguistic and institutional norms that keep them prisoners to a specific way of thinking that doesn't include the possibility of being with Jesus in the here and now. Again, I harken to laws, dogmas, and ideologies. Culture deceives us all into thinking that cultural norms are good and should be followed; and it is people of faith that suffer more than anyone else. When it comes to prayer, we are directed to avoid prayer of the heart because it is viewed as trying to escape the control that culture administers over the people, and when entering the realm of the unconscious people, in modernity belief you are open to evil spirits, etc.

Prayer of the heart is going beneath our conscious mind to allow the presence of the divine to speak and guide us. In short it is becoming closer to our instincts but more profoundly to have the experience of the divine in our life in a way that is more real to us than anything we experience in this world. Some of this bias comes from people with

[123]

mental diseases where medications are used to anesthetize the person and prevent unwarranted brain functions of the unconscious to emerge into a person's behavior. The major contributor to restraining mental prayer comes from religious institutions suggesting negative spiritual consequences when one has no control over their prayer, or at least no control from their perspective. To be trained to think in particular ways is not conducive to praying from the heart; we should always remember we cannot control the Holy Spirit, nor should we try. Perhaps the unforgiveable sin against the Holy Spirit might be denying his accessibility and encouraging others not to pray in ways that are of the heart. What the people in the valley were looking for was how to open their hearts to the presence of Jesus in the world we live in, not to meet him when they die.

I already spoke a bit about what ***Walking on the water*** symbolizes. But for me, the miraculous nature of Jesus' physical presence and walking on water, is like the miracle of him walking into a person's life, particularly mine. I didn't know at the time the potency of experiencing the person of Jesus. Intellectual experiences of Jesus are good, but their influential power is nothing compared to touching His hand. There is more practical theology revealed in the act of touching Jesus' hand because you are experiencing divine love, God, than everything that has ever been written about Him. Touching the hem of Jesus' garment was sufficient to heal the woman who hemorrhaged for 12 years. This incident in the Gospel of Luke 8:40-49, was not about Jesus having the intent to heal her. He wasn't aware of her presence until she touched the hem of His garment; but His presence was enough. Over time I came to realize this reality. I realized that meeting Jesus leaves an indelible mark on the person's psyche.

However, Jesus' presence can also have the opposite effect and leave an indelible mark, again on the psyche. In the first chapter of the Gospel of Mark Jesus is in a synagogue when a man with unclean spirit began shouting while Jesus was teaching on the scripture that was being read. The man who was shouting said, "What have you to do with us, Jesus of Nazareth? Have you come to destroy us? I know who you are, the Holy One of God." This person who met the person of Jesus, even though he was in a synagogue and supposedly a good Jew worshipping God, recognized who Jesus was (Luke 8:40-49). Jesus' bodily presence brought the unclean spirit out of the man; it left an indelible mark on the person, something that I witnessed at times while praying with people over the years. Evil is uncomfortable when in the presence of the divine or a person who presents the person of Jesus in their person.

13

Feed my Sheep

After the vision of being on the lake with Jesus, I felt the need for additional clarity as to what Jesus asked me to do. I understood it from an intellectual perspective, but Jesus didn't have to bless me with a vision for me to understand what he asks all Christians to do; that is, witness the gospel to the world. It seemed to me that there was more to the vision and its symbolism than I intellectually understood. I prayed and reflected on the vision, but it seemed that I was being asked to bring his people to him in a concrete or non-abstract manner. I was not certain what that meant. I intellectually understood what it meant to *"feed my sheep"* but the depth and width of what Jesus was asking was still a mystery, or at least foggy and not crystal clear, especially as it concerns the feelings I had that Jesus was asking me to bring his people to him in a concrete or non-abstract reality.

Over the next three years I routinely fasted for extended periods (a practice I maintained for most of my adult life) and prayed for clarification of what it meant to *"feed my sheep."* In the vision Jesus seemed to ask me to bring his people to him in an intimate and personal relationship which was unlike what the people in the vision were experiencing. These people accepted Jesus as their personal savior, but their faith resided more in their intellect than in their heart. They desired true communion with Jesus in the land of the living and in heaven. What was missing for them was to have Jesus, who brings them salvation through the forgiveness of their sins and eternal life, to reside as a real person in their heart, in a manner like the apostles did after the resurrection.

During Lent I had been fasting for about a week. One night while asleep, I heard a loud voice calling my name. The voice seemed to be right next to me. At first, I was shocked that somebody was in my bedroom in the middle of the night, but as I looked to see who was calling me, I didn't see anyone. My wife was asleep, and she is a rather light sleeper. It was obvious she did not hear the voice. I immediately turned my thoughts towards the calling of Samuel by God. After he called my name a second time I said, "Your servant is listening Lord." This very authoritative and yet loving masculine voice said, "Get up, go into your office and write what I tell you." I got up, went into my office and this is what the voice said:

"My son, you are to carry a torch through the darkness to light the way for my people.

If one is naked, clothe him with my Spirit.

If one is hungry feed him with my word, if in prison set him free.

If captive conquer his master and give him a new life.

If one be sick give him my love and heal his body that he may live.

Forgive my people their sins for I have given to you the power to recognize evil.

Do not judge my people but love my people.

[127]

Do not fear my people but give to them as I give to you.

Do not be apathetic to my people but compassionate.

The light you carry is the light of life and you will not know where you are going; for you must walk in faith.

It is not for you that you carry the light but for those who see it and follow you.

To carry a light of this type will not be easy but know that it is I who am with you.

I love you.

This is how you will feed my sheep."

I finished writing what the voice told me and went back to bed as if nothing had happened. When I woke up in the morning, I told my wife I had a strange dream. I went into my office to find on my desk my letter from God. I read it and I was overwhelmed with emotion. I was unable to read it again for over three years.

At first, when I considered the "feed my sheep" vision and then the contents of this locution, I was struck on the biblical nature of the verbiage. Then after many years of study, I became more educated about what it meant to have concrete and non-abstract behaviors. In my studies on symbolism, the psyche, and particularly the unconscious contents of the mind, as well as Old Testament language and ideas, it demonstrated a concreteness of language, the language of ancient humanity. These encounters with God were of the same nature. This observation has been important throughout my ministerial life.

This book is my reflection of how I am to carry the **Torch** of Jesus, the light of the world. The process of discovering that was one of already carrying His torch and a great blessing had occurred. I didn't understand what His torch was and how I would carry it until many years after the visions. My initial response and reflection on my letter from God, for me, was about my failures in serving Him. I received a great gift, and I was not doing all I could to fulfill His request, even though I didn't fully understand His request. It seemed to me to be far outside of my skills and faith level. I also understood to publicly witnessing His gift and fulfilling His request was likely to make me, in some fashion, a public figure of which I was deeply terrified.

My greatest sin, fear, is notoriety that might come by witnessing His great gift to me. I have never figured out why Jesus would ask me to carry His torch into the darkness because He knows my weaknesses and fears, but intellectually I know we are all sinners, and no one is righteous or holy enough to carry such a torch. I also realize Jesus did not just call me, but He has called many to carry his torch in the darkness of the world. I am a sinner who looks to my own needs before the needs of others and especially my Lord's desire for His people to know Him in a personal and intimate relationship. I am lacking in His love and the love for His people. I am not a special person or a righteous or holy person; spiritually different than most, but not special. I was once told that I am special because He gave me wonderful gifts and people don't receive letters from God every day. My response was, God gives us all gifts according to His will and pleasure, and no one is worthy to receive any gift from our Lord. Such a statement by that person about being holy only re-enforced my fear that others would see me as special, and I can assure everyone I am but a poor sinner who is full of weaknesses and fears. My task is to strengthen my faith to the point of allowing Jesus to do His work through me.

[129]

To carry a ***torch into the darkness,*** I believe is the light of Truth symbolized by a Torch. This is a common Christian symbol, as well as other religious symbols that illuminates the love of the divine to a world living in darkness. This darkness is not just overt sins of racism, hatred, war, politically motivated hunger, and disease, or the like, but also more subtle sins such as social propaganda, society's inducing fears and control over others, generally presented as a good. There is also the sin of those who accept cultural lies; that is, laws, dogmas, and ideologies. However, this torch is also about the darkness in our heart that is the result of the postulated lies noted above. Our heart is contaminated with worldly falsehoods that speak more to the Father of Lies than to the Truth of the divine. Such contaminated hearts are either closed or only slightly opened to the Truth, but to the degree they are occupied with lies, the person is a prisoner and slave to the dictates of the lie. I think the Torch I am to carry is to enter the heart and illuminate the darkness so that a person can enter a new freedom. This is the principal reason people have so much difficulty praying in a way that brings them into an encounter with Jesus, including myself.

In our religious world there is an ongoing bias between denominations ascribing it as the one true faith, which from its onset will create a form of religious elitism, even if it is well intended. The biggest Christian religious teachings are that Jesus is Lord and salvation comes to the believer in Jesus as the Son of God whose passion, death and resurrection redeemed us from sin and brings us into eternal life. Next is achieving knowledge about Jesus through scripture, sermons, formal teaching, or dogmas, and through discursive prayer. The problem is all these religious dogmas, well intended, are grounded in abstract interpretations, resulting in many truths, when there is but one Truth. I am

[130]

sure each institutional dogma will claim they are the actual truth.

All these dogmas are helpful but only tend to reinforce abstract ideas of Jesus. Intellectual prayer is good because it can prepare us to open our heart for the realization of indwelling of the spirit of the divine and the desire for the person of Jesus. However, there are a variety of obstacles that retard coming into the personhood of Jesus in our heart. These, I believe, are represented by the people in the valley praying for Jesus with their hands outstretched pleading for Jesus to come to them when they don't realize they are the ones that have to come to Him, just as the woman that hemorrhaged for 12 years. Remember that the divine gives us free will and respects his gift eternally. The Torch illuminates the obstacle(s) created by false assumptions and Jesus, with the consent of the person, overcomes the obstacles that are created by lies.

If one is naked clothe him with my Spirit: There are behaviors that separate us from each other, the divine that creates shame within us, the same shame and guilt that Adam and Eve experienced and pushed them away from God. Because of our shame we are reluctant to face the divine because our sins, even if unknown, naturally produce guilt, and the shame of our guilt drives us away from the divine. The same thing is true when we behave in a "separating" fashion with others. This is against the universal law of the divine. Jesus' bodily presence allows the person to experience his love and acceptance by removing shame and allowing a closer relationship with his Father. My task, in accordance with the spirit, is to bring people from the world of lies and falsehoods that we live in so that Jesus can overcome their shame. From a psychological perspective when there is shame there is guilt and the psychological necessity to be punished. Unless

[131]

shame is reconciled, punishment follows, either intellectual, emotional, or physical. At times all three forms of punishment may occur. The ultimate punishment is the destruction of the soul, but our Father's love is greater than any form of punishment.

If one is hungry feed him with my word: To be hungry means we lack that which physically sustains us, food. Jesus tells us, "Man shall not live on bread alone, but on every word that comes out of the mouth of God (Matthew 4:4)." This scripture verse was particularly important to me during a period of fasting. I understand this to mean that all people are hungry for the divine, but many are being sustained on lies and not on the Bread of Life. At times when praying with someone, I use a specific verse(s) or image(s) from scripture to facilitate an encounter with the person of Jesus. It makes no difference if the person is familiar with the verse or not because in prayer the image speaks to them in ways that convey the divine in the exact manner they need it. My experience is that in some manner the Word of God is satisfying to the soul.

If in prison set him free: For me, this verse isn't referring to being in jail or prison, or even a political prisoner. It is rather those ideas and or concepts that a person has made part of his or her world view that keep him or her from coming into the presence of Jesus. This is about what makes us a prisoner in our mindsets that affect our spirit, such as ideas, philosophies, institutional dogmas or laws, or customs that are preventing us to be open in a spirit of freedom and to come to the person of Jesus. The kingdom of the divine is a place in our heart where life is in contact with the divine.

Some cultural lies are forced on us, as if they are truths and must be lived in a prescribed manner set out by the law, dogma, or ideology. This is to keep people in the prison that

[132]

is designed by these false beliefs. If we venture off the plantation, the cultural, political, or institutional police will exact punishment to any offender with a variety of social weapons to force compliance. This is part of our cultural civil war that the United States and many countries are experiencing today.

What type of lies do we find in the American culture but also in all the communistic and socialistic governments? A good example is the idea that a woman has the right to determine what she will do with her body. On the surface this sounds life giving and in the spirit of advancing human freedom. However, it is used as a propaganda tool for a political platform that has an agenda that directly has nothing to do with the stated goal of freedom for a woman's right to choose. The goal that is not stated is, in fact, to make women slaves, not on the cotton plantations of an early era but slaves of political ideology of power, which like Jim Crow Laws are designed as subtle forms of subjugation. It is racism in its highest form. For those who buy into this ideology directly or support it, it is no different than any slave master or those who support slavery.

The idea of a woman aborting her baby was first postulated to racially eliminate or greatly reduce the number of black Americans by white racists. This concept was hijacked by those seeking to free women from the home to pursue careers as part of a sexual liberation philosophy for women, which was an attack on the family. It is a philosophy fostered by so-called elites whose message was primarily propagandized in major cities. Women were created to not just have children but to be the one that binds the family together. Marriage is on the decline and having children is on an even greater decline. These are all cultural lies that will destroy the soul because we are created to be creatures that are part of a family, to say nothing about the

[133]

destruction of culture. What will happen to these people, men and women, who have accepted these lies as they get older and more and more lonely? Satan knows to destroy the instinctual disposition of women will also destroy men, without even having to attack men. Such ideology emasculates men as central to being head of the house and provider for its security. This is perhaps the greatest sin and assault against our instincts; it will not be allowed as our instincts will rise and return humans to our instinctual goals.

Part of this newfound freedom was in the acceptance of the birth control pill and sexual revolution. This ushered in a new secular morality and civil laws allowing for abortion, the breakdown of traditional family structure, sexual preferences within the same sex, and the open use of drugs and a vocabulary of four-letter words as the common form of speech. So, we now see unbated crime without consequences, riots, and political sanctioning of a two-tiered system of laws, one for those who are following the laws, dogmas, and ideologies of the elites. If the state allows laws that are against natural law, it is still a sin. The state has never had, and never will have, the authority to determine what is good and what is evil. That is set by the divine and has been part of human behavior for millions of years.

These ideologies are being accepted by Christians and are leaving a deadly trail of wounded people, both men and women, but mostly women, and because these are the people who are the backbone of religions, it is destroying religions in the same manner. At one time, the prophets, and Jesus, and early Christians stood for Truth and did not back down from it, even if it meant going to the arena to face lions. Now we have far too many religious leaders that value their own life above their stated beliefs and do not publicly confront these laws, dogmas, and ideologies that are keeping the people of God from the desire of his heart. Who is worse? The one who postulates evil, or the one who knows that it is evil and allows souls to be destroyed? What would you say about a country whose laws permit the killing of its own citizens through abortion and creating a new moral standard through the state? I think it is appalling and the number of wounded souls is increasing every year. However, I have avoided the arena and am just as guilty. If I live to be 120 years old and am blessed with the ability to confront evil, I will, as I have finally decided to carry my Torch through the darkness regardless of the consequences.

Much of my ministry revolved around issues connected to the breakdown of the family. It leaves severe emotional wounds but also promotes a mindset that places the state above God who has already been the source of our morality. I have never been confronted with a woman who was trying to have an abortion, but I have met with women who have had abortions. Sometimes the woman believed she did the right thing because cultural dogmas told her to kill her own child so she could continue with her life without the baggage of a family. For her and the dogma, she is within her legal and moral rights, but she has incurred sin, and all sin produces guilt, and guilt produces the need for punishment. This is regardless of what our cultural laws say is legal. Other times they were filled with grief, shame, and emotional despair but culture will not help them because they are not compliant to the laws, dogmas, and ideologies that are being promulgated by false and egotistical self-proclaimed gods, the woke, and elites.

Women who felt shame and desired and longed for the Lord to forgive them and set them free from the emotional pain of intentionally taking a human life, especially her own baby, find little or no help from a godless world. Fifteen minutes in the presence of Jesus heals their wounds.

[135]

But there are those who would ask them to acknowledge they are a sinner and accept Jesus as their personal savior, which is good, but they are still left with their guilt, shame, and what will be their self-induced punishment. While there are others, very well-meaning people, who say you need to accept a dogmatic tradition to come to know the great love God has for you, this also is incredibly good, but the person is still left with their shame and in need for punishment. To cope with the pain, they may not seek the divine via a religion but seek forgiveness through the ideologies that promulgated the woman to have an abortion in the first place and might become involved in the rights of women to have abortions, with the idea that if everyone is doing it, it can't be wrong. They hope that their support of the lie will bring consolation with it. Unfortunately, it does not work, and the person becomes angry with those who do not support abortion, which generally means God.

I use the example of abortion because there is a push by some to legalize abortion everywhere. However, there are so many ways for a person to be in prison; that constitutes a book. One more example -- why are so many people so angry? We see anger and violence on social media that people gravitate to as if it were gold. Or we see violence on our streets and wonder why. Why are so many people today so angry? Why can't a person walk down the street at night in a city without feeling threatened? Crime is always a problem, but today walking down the main street in a large city is more a threat to the person's well-being than being a cowboy at the Okay Corral in Tombstone, AZ. I am in a prison when I cannot freely travel without the fear of being a victim of a crime, especially if I am on the wrong side of the political aisle. Any form of being in prison keeps us from seeking the divine because we are more concerned about our

[136]

own well-being, and rightly so. If I am being chased by a predator, I am focused on staying alive, whether that predator is an animal, person, law, dogma, or ideology.

If captive conquer his master and give him a new life: Who is the master in our life? If not God, then who? I suggest that if God is not our master, then Satan is, even if we are unaware of it. There is no neutral ground. In Revelation Chapter 3:15-16 we are told through the words of Jesus, "Because you are lukewarm, neither hot nor cold, I am about to spit you out of my mouth." This is not Jesus abandoning us, but I believe that to have a lived encounter with him, we cannot be living in two worlds. Remember, in the Book of Genesis, Satan is the most subtle of all God's creatures and that which he utters from his mouth are lies and most generally half-truths.

From my perspective, more than anything else, judging others separates us from others and the divine more quickly than anything else we can do. At the heart of judging is "feeling sorry for ourselves." By doing so we think of ourselves as superior to those we judge and, therefore, above the divine, although we don't typically recognize that we judge others. How difficult it is to have a conversation with friends without making some judgmental comments about someone during the conversation. It is not done in a malicious manner but nonetheless we judge the person because they are not there, and we are attempting to place ourselves above that person or situation. We judge in subtle ways, thinking we might even be helping others, or identifying evil within laws, dogmas, or ideologies. When we are involved with others and/or situations, we need to speak as truly as possible and infuse no moral superiority in our attitude. We should remember that Jesus reminds us that we judge by the flesh (human standards) but "I (Jesus) judge no one (John 8:15)." But we know that if He did judge, his judgment would not be like ours because He knows all things, and His battle is not with His people but with Evil who is attempting to destroy them.

You will see in the examples I cite that "judging" is a common theme and that when the person is set free from the pain of judging, that person obtains a new life. Judging is perhaps the most common sin we commit, generally unconsciously, but it reflects our unconscious position of moral superiority. As I noted above, the root of judging, as well as all other sins, is "feeling sorry for yourself."

If one be sick give to him my love and heal his body that he may live: I mentioned that there is more theology revealed by physically touching the hand of Jesus than any or all courses in theology. In his hand is divine love and love is God. To touch the hand of Jesus is to touch the hand of God, who is more than all theology combined. I am not referring to any description of touching the hand of Jesus that is in any way abstract but first and foremost is a tactile experience that your senses cannot deny. Such experiences do not occur in our visible and physical reality but in prayer of the heart, the reality of the heart. Love provides forgiveness of sin and removes our shame and guilt which then provides for healing the body and at times also saves the person, not the abstract salvation we have because of the passion, death, and resurrection but the salvation brought by the hand of Jesus as recorded in the scriptures.

Divine love is more powerful than anything humans have ever created, and God desires that we all experience his love in this world, as well as the next. I have no control over who will be healed by the Lord or when. What I know is that Jesus comes to those according to his will and not my will. I am normally just as surprised as the person who meets Jesus, in the same manner as the Apostle Paul did on the road to Damascus.

[138]

Forgive my people their sins for I have given to you the power to recognize evil: This verse is confusing for me. The forgiveness of sin I understand, and I can forgive those who assault, ridicule, and insult me. This verse seems to have a more universal nature to it. When I prayed with people, sin is part of the images portrayed within prayerful visions. As these are generated and guided by the Spirit, I assume that any forgiveness that takes place, because Jesus is present, implies forgiveness is from the divine. While the divine wants people to be free from sin to be completely on the path to him, he needs his people to act in his stead, but not from some form of dogma, which is not bad, but from the lived experience of Jesus laying his hand on the person and telling them that their sin is forgiven. They know experientially that God has intervened and forgiven that which they thought was impossible. One of the characteristics of sin is being subtle and difficult to recognize and therefore to forgive. When we see behaviors or speech that reveals that a person "feels sorry for himself," there is always the presence of sin.

Another characteristic of sin is its universality. We seem to be part of any sin, whether it is my sin or someone else's. To change our heart requires time and much focus for the goal of overcoming, meaning forgiving our sins, or an extraordinary amount of psychic energy to be released from within our emotional system. This is what happens when a person in prayer encounters the person of Jesus. Seeing and interacting with the divine releases massive amounts of psychic energy that can alert neural encoding that occurred with negative behaviors, that is called sin. The latter is what is occurring with people who I pray with when they encounter the person of Jesus. Tremendous psychic energy is released, and at times miracles occur, the greatest of these is the forgiveness of sin. I understand this type of

[139]

forgiveness as universal in nature, which is instinctual, and what I believe in the phrase, *Forgive my people their sins for I have given to you the power to recognize evil* means, but still leaves me wanting for further clarification.

Do not judge my people but love my people: I spoke briefly about judging above and why I think, on the surface, it is the deadliest sin. Connected to judging is the emotional sin of "feeling sorry for yourself." This is an insidious and very subtle way to separate ourselves from Jesus. As we make ourselves the center of the universe, we push God to the sidelines. We become the subject and object within our life or at least in part of our life. My understanding is not to judge because it is impossible to love the one you are judging. One might say 'I love my parents', but if I have judged them and it is unreconciled, then I cannot love them. So, my Father is saying to me that he wants me to love his people above all else, and to do so I cannot judge them.

Do not fear my people but give to them as I give to you: This verse is about me and my weaknesses; that is, my sins. I do fear the people of God. What I fear is making myself a public figure, losing my anonymity, especially with those who are in authority in the Roman Catholic Church. I am not sure what the Church may think about this book. They may think I am challenging accepted dogma; on that point I am not, and my personal faith is well within accepted dogma. I am however, concerned about a lived relationship with Jesus in a non-abstract reality and not a theological construct. Also, it is impossible to fear anything without first passing judgment on them or it, as I just discussed. For me, we are already in eternity having entered eternity before we were conceived. I fear that I will be misunderstood because they will think they cannot control me; they would be correct on that point. I cannot deny what I see, hear, or touch and I know Jesus is here right now. We cannot control when a person meets Jesus and wants to have an intimate relationship with him before we die and after. What I have experienced is from God and for his people, and while I benefit from my education and prayers with people, my life's experience cannot be taken away even if others attempt to discredit who and what I am or what I say.

There will be non-Catholics and Catholics alike who will not believe me and what I am revealing throughout this book, and likely will result in attacks and unwarranted judgments and belittling. Now that my wife is with Jesus, their attacks will be annoying but nothing else. I assume that theologians and academics will want to make their pronouncement about ideas and concepts laid out in this manuscript. This verse will be very helpful in keeping me from fighting back or judging them. Most of what I am discussing is about our psychology and that which is religious in nature is data for my psychological discussions, which is grounded in millions of years of evolution. Those who want to disagree with what I am saying, that is their prerogative, as no matter what they say cannot change my interaction and the relations others have had with Jesus.

Do not be apathetic to my people but compassionate: On the surface this verse sounds relatively easy, but this is an issue that is connected to my personality. My introversion is a problem for reaching out to others and my personality is also strongly analytical, so it is exceedingly difficult to be non-analytical when being compassionate. Also, my personality is non-apathetic because I can easily create distance between me and others. This verse is about my spiritual growth and my need to have a more complete and fully developed personality. God created me so he knows me through and through, and the difficulties I have dealing with the emotions of others. My time as chaplain helped me greatly in working on this issue but I am a slow

[141]

learner, and my weakness is very strong. I need to be compassionate not only to others but myself as well.

I never wanted to become a deacon in the Church because I knew that my weaknesses would be tested, and I did not want to be tested. However, after many years of kicking up my heels, I gave in to God's hounding my spirit and I decided to serve Him as a deacon. This was not good enough and my offer to serve Him as a deacon didn't seem to be enough as I was still being hounded. I had to agree to serve him for my entire life, 24 hours a day, and 365 days a year. It wasn't until we came to that agreement that He stopped hounding me. This, like several other events, reminded me of the saying 'I will dedicate my life to God.' In the backseat of a 1954 Ford at the age of 14 I had no idea what I was agreeing to. I pray for a long life so I can serve my Father as his servant.

The light you carry is the light of life and you will not know where you are going; but you must walk in faith: I understand the light of life to be the Word of God; that is Jesus. My experiences of Jesus and being with others is an honor beyond words. I am an unworthy servant, a doula for Jesus. To be accepted into his workplace, the fallen world of Eden, and to bring his people closer to him is an honor beyond words, but I am not worthy of such a calling as I am weak and not strong enough to stand up against laws, dogmas, and ideologies. However, even in my weaknesses Jesus still uses my gifts for the renewal of his people's soul. At times the same Jesus of Galilee heals their physical, emotional, and psychological wounds giving them a new life. He does this through forgiveness of sin and at times will save the person. By this I am not speaking about eternal salvation, which he does for all who call upon his name but saves their personality from destruction; he, at times, resurrects their soul and at other times he heals the wounded

[142]

personality. To witness these miraculous or divine actions is more than an honor; it leaves me in awe. I wish his forgiveness was being experienced by everyone, but Jesus will not work against a person's will.

If a person chooses not to be with Jesus in this world or at least deepen their relationship with him, Jesus remains faithful, a faithfulness that goes beyond the veil of death. I can testify that I never knew what the Lord had for me to do, nor when, how, or why I was going to do it. My task was always to be open to the Holy Spirit's guidance in all situations. This is not easy in a world focused on Evil.

My ministries and ecclesiastical assignments as a deacon were, of course, conducted in the same manner. I never refused or asked for any ministry. For 40 years I just did what I was asked to do, and I prayed that I didn't mess it up too much. I typically worked 65 hours a week to do what I was asked to do. Now my time of being a servant for Jesus is slowing down in what I can do physically, as a factor of age and Post Polio Syndrome is increasingly preventing me from standing, but for a minute or so, and walking is difficult. Nerve damage causes a diminishing ability for balance, and I am concerned about falling. However, if asked, I will do the best I can.

The phrase in this verse, "but you must walk in faith," is the key to my spiritual problem; the key word is faith. The Nicene Creed speaks about things we accept as true but cannot always prove them. Or a similar approach to faith is to believe in things hoped for but in our lack of faith we seek assurance of that which we don't see. But these normal definitions do not satisfy my soul. What does satisfy my soul are my memories and the heavenly treasures I experienced being with Jesus.

I have chosen from my own free will to live my life and to die as the willing servant of my Father, Jesus, and the

[143]

Holy Spirit. I still do not know where I am going, save to heaven, in this world but I will do the best I can to comply with what Jesus asks of me.

It is not for you that you carry the light but for those who see it and follow you: This verse frightens me down to my soul but also excites me more than I can explain. The reason it frightens me is my fear of becoming a public person and especially for others to think I am special. The truth is, I sin, and any sin is sufficient to separate us from God for eternity, unless we confess the sin, ask for forgiveness, and be reconciled with God, now or in the next life. I am no better than the worst of all sinners. We all need forgiveness and acceptance of his love. Notoriety is not unknown to me, and I was very uncomfortable when I was front and center. I delight in the possibility that I can have a small part in leading the people to Jesus and he can be in a person's life in a physically experiential way. It is Jesus who heals, it is Jesus that restores life where life is damaged, and it is Jesus who saves now and in eternity. It is my task to help the souls of those Jesus sends to me to have an intimate physical experiential relationship with the person of Jesus in the here and now, and when that occurs, thanks be to God.

I don't seek to be the light, but to carry it for others to see and to follow the light is more than amazing. It is to touch the hand of the creator of the universe who is the humblest of all beings. I am struck with the humility of Jesus; he is not intimidated by sharing his personhood with others.

To carry a light of this type will not be easy but know that it is I who am with you: This is a wonderful verse for my spiritual well-being. I can testify that over 40 years of ecclesiastical ministry has in no way been easy. I abhor politics in the Church, unavoidable, but I seem to have been deeply involved and struggled against becoming part of it. I

[144]

know that without my letter from God, I am sure I would have succumbed to the political power or influence and become institutionalized. I am proud of only one thing that I did on my own and it was not to give in to the temptation of political power.

I am opening more and more to everyone I meet, but this is very hard and virtually unknown to me. This book is an example of being open to the world. I am still not good at being open to others as it is a new part of my personality. To be more personable is very difficult and most of the time it is not normal, and I avoid it. It is a characteristic of Jesus that he uses to draw others to himself, something I should greatly improve on in my life, especially when carrying such a great light.

I love you: To hear these three words is unbelievably and profoundly the most meaningful words I have ever had addressed to me, especially because they were spoken by the creator of the universe: incredible! It is also why I had such an emotional response when I read my letter from God the next day and why I could not read it or teach it for about three years. To think that the creator of the universe knows me by name and that he loves me is all I need in my life. I love my wife, children, and family who mean the world to me, but I still can't get over that my Father spoke to me. I know him in my place of peace but not in the way I know him after he spoke to me asking me to serve him in a specific manner.

This is how you will feed my sheep: I know I am not a good servant, and I know I still sin, but I also know I do whatever I can to fulfill his request. At times I do better than at other times, but I try. On my tombstone all I want is "I lived, I died, I tried."

[145]

[Each of the remaining episodes are about encounters I had with Jesus, while praying with others. In Chapter 28 are guidelines on praying by ourselves to have an encounter with Jesus.]

EPISODE 6
Spiritual Healings

14

The Woman who Aborted her Child

This is an example of setting a person free from their prison of guilt, also a person who truly sought forgiveness. It is the divine who knows our heart and it is our heart that speaks the truth, even when we are unaware of it, and the divine who knows the contents of our heart's response to our prayer.

This event happened while I was a hospital chaplain. Note how the Spirit knows what is in her heart, is guiding the woman to me, and how he chose me to be part of her healing. This is about a wounded heart, a wound that only Jesus can heal with his love, how the Holy Spirit used me as his instrument of healing.

A woman was on her way to the grocery store which was about a mile from the hospital. As she was approaching the hospital, she had an overpowering need to stop at the hospital. She parked but didn't understand why she was there. She decided to leave and go to the grocery store as planned. She began pulling out of her parking spot when again was compelled to go into the hospital. She went in but had no idea why. After about a half hour she saw the chaplain's office and knocked on the door. When I opened the door, she told me the story of how she got to my door. She was a Methodist but had not been to church in over 20 years. She stopped going to church in the 1960s, she was in her 40s and never married. After hearing her story, I said, "Like you, I have no idea why you are here, but would you like to pray?" She said, "Yes!"

As I began to pray with her, she immediately entered a vision. I could see and hear everything in her vision, as if I was the one having the vision. The vision was taking place in a small pre-Vatican II Catholic chapel, prior to 1965. She sat down on the left side of the nave in the fifth pew from the front. There was a full-size statue of the Virgin Mary behind the altar rail and to the left of the altar. I expected to see a statue of Joseph on the right side but there was no statue. There also wasn't a tabernacle in the sanctuary. I thought this was strange for a Catholic chapel not to have a statue of Saint Joseph or a tabernacle. Standing next to Mary was a statue of a young male about three years old who I thought was a young Jesus with his mother Mary.

I asked her to walk up to the altar rail towards Mary, as this was the only thing that stood out in the vision. She got four or five feet from the rail and the statue of Mary came to life and picked up the statue of the child and the statue of the young boy also came to life. The woman stopped and was shocked that the statues were coming to life, as was I. Mary walked up to the rail while still holding the child. The woman exclaimed, "That's my baby!" Mary said, "I have been taking care of him until you could come." Mary then gave the child to the woman and as the woman received her baby, Jesus was standing at her side and Mary disappeared. I could not hear what the woman was saying to her baby, but it seemed to be very joyful emotions. After she finished saying all that she wanted to say to her baby, she turned to Jesus and gave him her baby, who said to her, "Now I will care for him until you come to take care of him."

[150]

With that, Jesus began to ascend with the baby in hand. I could see the ceiling of the church open to the sky as Jesus and the baby continued to ascend into the sky. The sky itself opened to heaven and I could hear choirs of angels, the hosts of heaven, and saints all singing praises to Jesus. The sound was indescribably magnificent. Jesus and the baby entered, and the heavens closed. The vision came to an end.

The woman opened her eyes and just stared as she seemed to be reorienting herself to this world. I asked her if she was okay and she replied, "I am all better now." She went on to tell me that she got pregnant when she was 18 years old. She also said she was deeply involved in the sexual revolution of the 1960s and was told by her friends and culture that having an abortion was a good thing to do because the fetus is not a person, she wasn't married, and it wasn't immoral because abortion is legal; she lived in a state that had just repealed abortion laws. She noted how she was always haunted by what she did and emotionally suffered greatly; so, at the time she got more involved with the sexual revolution hoping that it would make her feel better, but it didn't comfort her. She got out of the politicization of abortion, but she continued to have emotional issues. She never married because she thought if she got pregnant it would be disrespectful to the baby who was aborted. She left and I never heard from her again.

I want to point out that the woman had a grievous sin, but Jesus knew what was in her heart and he saved her because of his presence to her and his love for her was sufficient to overcome her sin. In her old reality, a reality that imposed itself on life with several lies, her baby was dead and because of her sin she too was emotionally dead. But she must have prayed fervently not only for her baby but for the divine to hear her prayers and answer them. She knew Jesus had forgiven her because He was there and did

[151]

not condemn her and he said, "Now I will care for him until you come to take care of him." I also found it strange she was in a Catholic Church with its statues and the altar separated from the people by an altar rail. Even more telling was the image of Mary who was taking care of her baby. Typically, Methodists are not strong on praying to Mary. I don't know if she prayed to Mary or not, but I know Mary was instrumental in her healing. These are not the images of the Methodists, but they are images from within her heart, guided by the Spirit. She was a slave to the effects of ideologies. She was no longer agreeing with the idea about killing of babies in the womb but never became reconciled with the divine, so she remained a prisoner, but Jesus set her free from that which kept her in bondage for many years. God is good.

15

The Woman whose Father Died

This example is when I was a chaplain, and how Jesus always is moving towards reconciliation either with sin or in relationships. This example is of Jesus interceding to make sure a wonderful relationship continued.

I met a woman in intensive care whose father had just died the previous day. Her mother died at home twenty years earlier, and her father moved in with her and her family. She was very close to her father, and he was very grateful that he was living with her, his son-in-law, and his grandchildren. By the time I met her the grandchildren were no longer living there; they had children of their own but were still very close. The entire family was very supportive of each other; it was refreshing to see such a loving family.

She was the caregiver for her father. He was so pleased with how he was treated, and for years he told her how grateful he was and when he died, he was going to take her with him. When he died paramedics got there only to find that the woman had also gone down from shock. She thought that because her father died, she was going to die as well, since that is what her father told her for years, "When I die, I will take you with me." Her father stayed at the house because he was dead, and the paramedics called the coroner. The woman was admitted to intensive care because the doctors felt she was undergoing physical issues with her heart due to tremendous stress from her father dying. For the next several days the woman remained in ICU at which time I visited her routinely because of the stress she was experiencing. The family was also with her most of the time because they all believed she too might die, because of what her father said. After about a week the family scheduled the funeral for the next day, several days after she was transferred to a medical floor where her heart could be monitored. I asked whether she would like me to be with her at the time of the funeral, and I could do memorial prayers for him in her room. She said yes, and her granddaughter, who was in her 20's, decided not to go to the funeral because she felt her grandmother would need emotional support. I began the memorial prayers and both the granddaughter, and the woman closed their eyes and held hands as I was praying. Suddenly, and without any prompting on my part, or without any thoughts about having an encounter with the person of Jesus, he appeared to both the woman and her granddaughter, and me even with my eyes open to continue reading the prayers.

They were both seeing precisely the same thing as I was. At first, Jesus was just present until I finished the memorial prayers, about several minutes. When I finished the prayers Jesus and now her father were present. Now Jesus and the woman's father came to the woman and her granddaughter's great grandfather, and they were allowed to say their goodbyes. Jesus and her father thanked her for her loving and compassionate care of her father. Jesus and the man began to ascend, as the ceiling opened, then the skies, and then heaven opened to choirs of angels, the host of heaven, and saints all singing praises to the Lord. The heavens closed and the vision was over. The woman and her granddaughter just looked at one another as if they were

[154]

coming from a different reality. They spoke to one another about what they saw and what they saw was identical. They were dumbfounded.

The woman began walking through the hall and telling everybody that she saw Jesus. It was creating quite a stir, but the nurses were not able to slow her down. The family came back from the funeral thinking that the woman was going to be emotionally stressed out, but instead they found a woman who was so excited that they had difficulty slowing her down. They said, "Come into the room and we will tell you how nice the funeral was." She retorted, "No, I will tell you what really happened." The woman was discharged that afternoon.

16

The Woman who Ran over her Child

One afternoon I was called to the emergency room because a child of about 16 to 18 months old died after being run over by an automobile. As a chaplain, I dreaded having to respond to the death of young children. I felt helpless being unable to remove the pain of the parents. I wanted to be compassionate to them, but nothing was going to relieve their pain, at least that's what I thought before this event.

The situation reported by the paramedics was that the mother of the child in our family room was backing her car out of the driveway when the child suddenly ran towards the car. Before anyone who was in the yard with the child was able to prevent the child tripping and falling under the rear wheel of the car, resulting in the mother running over her baby. It turned out that the mother of the child was on her way to the store and the child was outside playing with several brothers and his sister along with his father and as she pulled out of the driveway, he got underneath the car, and she ran over the child killing him. The paramedics decided to take the child to the hospital where they knew the family could get immediate support until the victim advocate could be mobilized. This decision that the paramedics made was not in compliance with normal protocols, for when a person dies away from a medical facility the body is to remain in place for the coroner. God was at work even with the paramedics.

When the family arrived, they already knew the child was dead. I went to the family room and the child's mother and father, and three brothers and one sister were in the room. The entire family was quite distraught, especially the child's mother who was driving the car. Everyone felt remorse and guilt for what happened. It was as if each person was on an island by themselves, each one was alone with their sorrow, grief, and guilt. I felt so sorry for them, and helpless to truly be able to help them. It is so sad to witness events like this, for me and for the medical staff, to say nothing about the family. When I got into the room and saw what the family was going through, I didn't know what to do.

I asked if the mother would like to pray, and the entire family agreed. As we began to pray, I immediately, in my mind, saw Jesus standing with her. Jesus was next to the mother of the child and holding the child with very loving care. I could not hear what Jesus was saying to the mother, but whatever Jesus said, the woman who was now holding her baby was talking to the child and the child seemed to be at peace and surrounded by divine love, which the mother was being bathed in as well. She instinctually knew to give her child back to Jesus, and when she gave Jesus her child, Jesus, said, "I will take care of him," and he began to ascend toward heaven. The ceiling of the hospital opened, and then the heavens opened, and I could hear choirs of angels and saints and the host of heaven all singing praises to the Lord. The vision came to an end. Only the woman and I saw Jesus and what happened.

I was always amazed when someone died and I was part of their prayer, how Jesus would ascend into the heavens, how the heavens would open, and the choirs of angels, saints, and the host of heaven would all be singing praises to Jesus. These events were all the same but with different people.

By the time the prayer ended, everybody was still very distraught about what happened except for the mother of the child who was at peace and knew that her son was now with Jesus. She tried to tell them what happened in the vision, but they didn't believe her. She left the hospital very sad that her son was dead; she was also full of joy for having seen Jesus. However, the rest of the family were very traumatized. I was very puzzled as to why the rest of the family didn't encounter the person of Jesus as she did.

About three years later I happened to be a presenter for a national seminar on grief and the woman and her husband were at the seminar. She came up to me after the seminar and introduced herself and asked if I remembered her and her family. I did, how could I forget? I asked her how she was doing and how her husband and kids were doing. She informed me that was why they were attending the seminar. She was hoping to get help for them as they were still suffering. She missed her son greatly but was doing just fine because she knew where her son was and that he was in the best of all possible hands. Whenever she thought of her child that died, she experienced the love of God in her heart and his peace and joy. Encountering the person of Jesus provides healing and peace and a joy that surpasses our understanding. I pray that the rest of the family got help and was able to live without the emotional burden of guilt.

17

The Woman who Saw Paradise

I was visiting a woman in the hospital who had cancer of the liver, and was dying, likely within about a week. She was terrified of dying. When I asked her why she was frightened, her reply was, "I don't know if there is eternal life, and I am not sure if there is life after death if I would go to heaven. I was a practicing Christian for most of my life and thought I believed but now I am facing death, and I don't know if I truly believe, but I am coming to understand that to just believe what I was told about heaven is not enough for me, because in my belief is also my unbelief and that is what terrifies me. My family is very concerned about how terrified I am, but they don't understand; I am dying and very soon." Over the next five or six visits with her, we talked about her situation, and we prayed, but I never prayed in a way that could lead to the possible encounter with the person of Jesus. I just didn't sense I was to pray that way with her, and I have learned that when I tried to pray with someone because I wanted them to be healed, nothing would happen.

The last time I visited her I had the sense that Jesus wanted to come to her. I asked her if she wanted to pray, and she said yes, so I began to pray with her, and Jesus appeared to her. He didn't say anything, nor did she. He walked up to her; she was in her hospital bed. He took her by the hand, and she got out of bed and walked with him. The wall opened into another world, and Jesus led her into this world that was very beautiful, brilliant colors and pastoral landscape, with big, beautiful trees that I could not identify. Jesus turned to her and said, "This will be your new home soon, and I will be here to greet you." The short vision came to an end and the woman was a different person, no longer fearful of dying.

I never saw her again, but the nurse told me that she was completely different and at peace. Her family was very grateful that she was no longer terrified. She died the next day.

18

The Woman who Walked off into the Desert

This is an example of the divine respecting a person's free will and allowing them to continue their own path, if that is what they want. This is very difficult for me to understand as I always want people to be on the path and seeking the divine, but we are imbued with free will for a reason. From my perspective it is the only way we can freely choose to be with the divine as love is a function of free will.

I met this person while I was a chaplain, and she was a patient that routinely came into the hospital for all manner of complaints. Her doctor confidentially told me he believed her to be a hypochondriac but because he knew her as a surgical nurse before she retired, he tried to do what he could but was grateful that I was seeing her as he felt I was better suited to help her than he was. I saw her at least monthly for about three years, either in the hospital or at her home. She called me every day, mostly between 2 am and 4 am, and when I answered the phone all she did was sigh. After about 45 minutes and never speaking, she would hang up. She truly believed that it was God's fault that her husband died about ten years earlier. She never accepted his death and blamed God for his death. To say she was angry at God would be an understatement.

The last time I visited her we spoke about God, and she said that she loved him, but her actions just didn't seem to fit what she was saying. I asked her if she would like to pray and come into the presence of Jesus. Surprisingly she said yes. We started our prayer and immediately she was on a path. On her right side was an empty wasteland and on her left side were green fields with rolling hills with sporadic oak trees that seemed to be full of life. There were no animals or other forms of vegetation, only vibrant green grass, and oak trees. Suddenly, Jesus was standing next to her on her left. He said nothing, nor did she. They began to walk down this path and after about 25 yards, Jesus stopped, turned to her, and said, "You must choose." I heard what he said, as I was gifted to see and hear everything that was occurring in the prayer. I wasn't sure what he was referring to, as I was looking for anything that he was referring to. Choose what?

The woman didn't say anything nor did Jesus. In a very short time, the woman turned away from Jesus and walked out into the wilderness and the vision came to an end. I finally understood what Jesus was asking her and the image he used to ask the question, an image of emptiness, versus an image of life. When the prayer was over, I asked her why she chose to walk out into the emptiness of the wilderness. She said, "I felt compelled to walk that way as I didn't want to be with the one who took my only love in life away from me." At first I was deeply saddened by her comment, but after reflection I came to understand that wherever love is, God is present and even though she didn't realize this because of her woundedness and strong sense of "feeling sorry for herself" the divine is the divine and does not change. Where there is love, God is present, perhaps unseen or unrecognizable, but he is still there and at some point, the one who alienates himself from the divine will find he is and always has been standing at their side, regardless of time or space.

Three weeks later, after I saw her for the last time, I received a call from her older brother who informed me that she died. He said that he had spoken to her about a week before she died and she told him that she loved her husband and wanted to be with him, and if something happened to her, to tell me how much my visits meant to her as it was the only other time she experienced love, other than when her husband was alive. I knew that her love for her husband would lead her to the Father.

19

The Man in Torment and the Power of Prayer

Above I spoke about a patient in the hospital that had a vision of paradise when encountering the person of Jesus. In other examples, I spoke about how in some cases the heavens opened as Jesus was ascending into heaven. We could hear the choirs of angels, saints, and host of heaven all singing hallelujahs to Jesus. These events I report were all the same although witnessed by different people and in no way promoted by me, which I find fascinating and a very hopeful image for the afterlife. But all is not what it might seem. In this example I leave it to the reader to interpret this for yourself. It is gruesome. From my perspective, since the time of this event I have prayed for all the souls revealed in this vision, some of which are my relatives.

A person I routinely prayed with had a vision of a man standing in front of the person in the living room of their house. The man standing there had no head and wore a checkered shirt. The person who was praying wasn't praying for such an event but praying in general for others, and as one would suspect was freaked out by it. They asked the man who he was but got no answer. Then the man was asked why he was there. "To thank you, as we are all looking for prayer, as the way out of our place and your prayer was allowed to penetrate the darkness. I was able to get out of the darkness through the hole your prayer opened."

When asked where he was from, he said, "From the darkness that never ends, and we all are endlessly spinning around and around within the darkness looking for a small speck of light that we know is prayer of a righteous person and whose prayers can get us out of the place we are in and back on our journey to God." Asked why he didn't have a head and why he was wearing a checkered shirt? "We are all souls who lived a checkered life, and we must wear a checkered shirt to remind us of our self-centeredness and bad behaviors that hurt others, and I have no head because I blew it off in suicide." The soul of the man, again, said thank you for your prayers and left. The vision was over, and the person never saw the man in the checkered shirt again.

Prayer is more powerful than we understand. Prayer is good for the souls of those we pray for in this world or the next. The man in the checkered shirt said they are always looking for the prayer of a righteous person that will allow them to get out of the darkness that never ends. For me, it sounds like a hellish place but what I do know is that a righteous person is a person on the path and, therefore, is, to some degree, living in accord with the divine and their prayers are an image of the one praying. It can only be the will of the divine that will allow for such prayer to penetrate the endless darkness and allow for a soul to move on to get back onto the path. It is the will of the Father that all those who the Father gave to Jesus, that Jesus lose no one. From my perspective, this vision is testimony to John 6:37-40.

20

Jesus Carried their Cross

I visited a person at his home who I had seen many times. He had significant family issues that I was unable to resolve. The person had passed judgment on several members of the family who were living with them. Their judgments were about how the family never did what they wanted the family to do for them. In short, they were living a life of being the center of the universe, and it was obvious how "they felt sorry for themselves." The relationships were very dysfunctional, on the person's part and others in the family. I would always hear them tell me how others hurt them, and they had no desire to forgive and reconcile.

I tried several times to pray with the person to have a personal and lived encounter with Jesus but never was successful. It seems that it is Jesus who decides who he will have an encounter with and when, not me. This time I didn't have the intention of asking Jesus to be present to the person, but I just wanted us to pray as we began our session. As I started to pray, Jesus came to the person in a vision that we both saw in our heads. Jesus took the person by the hand and led him to a large enclosure that had no ceiling but had a porch about four feet above the ground level of the enclosure. There was one entry into this courtyard and stairs at one end of the courtyard that went up to the porch. At the end of the porch was a door that went inside an attached large building.

At first Jesus led them into the courtyard and they were alone. I could see and hear everything but wasn't part of the scene. Someone I didn't know, who looked to be a Roman Centurion, took the person to the stairs, and then locked the person in chains in the middle of the porch. A man of authority came out of the building and stood next to the person who was now in chains. He asked the crowd of people that had just appeared what he should do with this person. The response by the people was vigorously, "crucify, crucify." The man in authority asked the crowd why, what has he done to deserve such a penalty? But the crowd just continued to shout, "crucify, crucify."

The person was terrified, but the worst was yet to come. As the centurion took a whip to begin to flog, Jesus appeared, standing next to the person, and said, "This is too much for you; I will take your place." Now Jesus was the one in chains, and the person was observing Jesus being scourged for the faults of which the crowd was accusing the person.

After being whipped, Jesus was brought to the feet of the person and the man in authority turned to the crowd again and said, "See I have punished him, shall I now release him?" The response was, "crucify, crucify." Now Jesus, who was standing in for the person, was led into the area where the crowd was and was given a large timber to carry to his crucifixion. The person stood on the porch and watched as Jesus picked up the cross. As he began to walk out, the timber he was carrying hit the wall in the doorway and a small piece of the timber fell to the ground, a piece weighing no more than half an ounce. The person on the porch ran down to that speck of wood laying on the ground and knew that as part of his sins had to be part of the cross

[167]

Jesus was taking to the place of crucifixion for the forgiveness of sins. The person tried to pick up the sliver of wood but was not strong enough to pick it up. The weight of sin is enormous. Then Jesus came to the person and picked him up and said, "I told you that you are not strong enough for this; I will do it for you."

Jesus picked up the sliver and along with his timber went to a place outside of the town and the person watched as Jesus was crucified; it was the hammering of spikes into his hands and feet that the person found to be so horrifying. He died on the cross, but just before he died, he lifted his head towards heaven, "Forgive this person Father, they don't know what they are doing." He was placed in the tomb and people gathered around the tomb. They began to talk about the crucifixion but only was talking about Jesus, never mentioning the person, who became angered that he was not the center of attention and immediately Jesus was back at the place of his crucifixion and the soldiers were driving the nails into his hands and feet again. This repeated several times until the person no longer was passing judgment on those who were speaking about the death of Jesus. He learned not to be the center of attention by judging others.

The vision came to an end and the person was deeply sorrowful for his behaviors and the need to be the center of attention in the family. This began the long arduous journey of repentance of "feeling sorry for himself," and placing his needs over the others in the family. The family was slowly beginning to be repaired.

21

Those who Visited me at Mass

I had many encounters with the dead coming to me and my wife, Kathy, asking for prayer, mostly family members but at times people that knew us. Most of the time we would have our table lamp lights go on spontaneously. Within several hours or days, we would be notified of a family member dying, generally from out of state, and in some cases from Europe. Sometimes my wife or I would wake up at night to see someone standing at the foot of our bed. At no time would we hear them speak to us. We just knew they died and needed prayer.

As a chaplain I was with about 3,300 people who died. One day at Mass, during the readings and responsorial psalm, all the people in the church disappeared at the beginning of the first reading of the Old Testament, and suddenly I was the only person in the entire church. The priest I was sitting next to, the servers, and the choir were gone instantly. I thought I was having a stroke or something like that. Almost immediately all the doors opened, and people came in and sat down in the pews in an orderly and yet very quick fashion. Many people were unable to sit due to lack of seats. Those who could not sit stood at the sides and back of the nave of the church. With people standing in our nave there would be about 1,100 people.

The group of people that came in after sitting for a brief time just vanished. By that I mean they did not get up and walk out, they just vanished into thin air. As soon as they were gone, a second group came into the nave in the same manner as the first group; again, about 1,100 people. They too disappeared and after they disappeared a third new group came in of the same number. I was freaked out. My wife was at Mass, and she too disappeared with all the parishioners at the beginning of this vision. Finally, the third group disappeared and in an instant all the parishioners were back in their seats, as if nothing had happened.

When the first group came in and sat down, I was freaked out. The second group came in, and they seemed to be familiar, but I was unable to identify them. Finally, the third group came in and I knew who they were, and they all knew me. These were people who I was with when they died. I had the sense they knew me, but I was also confused because some of these people were unconscious or dead when I saw them, and normally when someone is in that state, they don't know anything, but that was not what I was experiencing; they knew me and, in some way, unknown to me. I felt they were thanking me or telling me that my prayer for them was not in vain or unheard. There were about 3,300 people there and I was with every one of them when they died. There is more to life, and perhaps death, than we understand.

EPISODE 7
Physical Healings

22

The Man with the New Heart Valve

This example occurred while I was visiting a patient whose nurse asked me to see him prior to having open heart surgery. The surgery to open three arteries and replace the aortic heart valve was scheduled for the next morning. The patient's healing occurred because of Jesus' great and unconditional love, and the patient's response to that love by reconciling with the patient's parents and grandparent. Also note in this example the effects of judging others, even when we have what we normally would call a "good reason." And as I have previously pointed out, sin is always an issue. Jesus moves towards reconciliation; regardless of the sin it unconsciously focuses us on the judgments of the sin and that separates us from the divine.

I met with this 38-year-old patient in Intensive Care at 6 o'clock in the evening for about two hours. I didn't spend much time discussing personal issues or concerns of the patient. I knew the patient was divorced and had two children that he rarely saw. He had no family or friends with him at the hospital. The patient did not have a religious preference, nor did he practice religion, even in the past, but believed in God and that Jesus was His only son.

I felt that the Spirit wanted me to pray with the patient, so I asked, "Would you like to pray?" The answer was "yes." As we began to pray, Jesus appeared to the patient almost immediately in a vision that I could see and hear what the patient could see and hear; although I only knew feelings and emotions by what I could observe. Jesus took the patient by the hand and took him to his childhood home, specifically to the kitchen. The patient saw his mother and father who the patient did not trust or even like. In fact, there was great hatred because the patient's father physically abused him until he was removed from the house by the state. He went to live with the father's mother who raised the patient from age 12 and the patient loved the grandmother dearly. The grandmother was not present in the kitchen, and I didn't learn about living with the grandmother until later in the vision. The patient loathed his mother because of her weakness in allowing her husband to abuse their child; the act of doing nothing was, for the patient, a bigger sin. The patient's mother, father, and grandmother were all dead.

While in the kitchen the patient got into a fist fight with the father that was quite violent and drew blood on each of them. The father was getting the worst of the fight when it just seemed to stop. I was perplexed as to why Jesus was standing there and allowed this to take place; it didn't fit my image of the Prince of Peace. However, Jesus allowed the donnybrook to continue until the patient beat the father but did nothing to the mother. The patient in the vision was his current age, 38 years old.

I asked the patient to forgive the father for what he had done while being abused by him. This was extremely difficult and required considerable time, but only partial forgiveness was occurring and more had to be done for complete and unconditional forgiveness. I asked the patient to move his sense of awareness into the mind of Jesus and to see his father as Jesus does. The patient was able to do this

[174]

and saw the father through the eyes of Jesus and the patient was moved with compassion and was able to forgive completely and unconditionally. I don't know what he saw as I was not privy to that event. However, it was reciprocal on the part of the father and the patient had a new relationship with the father; he was able to interact with his father in freedom and love.

I asked the patient to go to the mother and to forgive her as well, but it was necessary to repeat the same process that the patient had with the father. Eventually the patient was able to forgive the mother completely and unconditionally and to embrace her. The mother was now emotionally able to act at a new level of freedom with the patient and could now express her love. The mother and the father now seemed to have a new relationship with each other. It looked to me that Jesus had worked out reconciliation between all three and I expected the vision to come to an end.

I asked Jesus if there were any other issues that needed to be reconciled. Jesus responded by taking the patient by the hand again. He took him to a place that was very frightening for the patient, a place of total blackness. There was no light, no floor, no ceiling, no walls, no sounds, and no wind. It was as if we were in hell, very uncomfortable and unsettling. Jesus was there but no longer holding the patient's hand. I was there and my senses recorded nothing, save the presence of Jesus.

I asked the patient to ask Jesus why we were there. Immediately there was the appearance of a very small light, like a strobe light flashing in the dark. I asked the patient to move towards the light. Since there was no other light, it was impossible to determine the size or the distance we were from the light. When the patient got there, it turned out to be a very small jewel, about the size of half a dime in diameter. It appeared to be as transparent as a diamond. The jewel was still producing light when I asked the patient to look very closely at the object. As the patient gazed at the object, the patient could see the face of somebody inside of it. The patient said, "Her face is very ugly and frightening; it is a witch." I asked the patient to allow the witch to come out of the object.

During this period neither of us could see nor hear Jesus, although we felt his presence. As the witch appeared, the patient recognized the witch as the patient's grandmother who raised him. As it turned out, the patient hated the grandmother more than the patient's father or mother because it was the patient's grandmother that allowed her husband (the patient's grandfather) to physically abuse the patient's father. The amount of emotional hatred for the grandmother was palpable and the patient wanted to destroy her. This was all very confusing because this was the only person in the family the patient loved but this love was based on the patient's survival and not on actual love. The patient never experienced unconditional love, nor did he ever know his grandfather who abused his father; he died before he was born. Now the patient was left with the same problem, reconciling with the grandmother. Going through the same process, the patient became reconciled with the grandmother, and then the father, mother, and grandmother all became reconciled; perhaps the first time they were experiencing unconditional love. After that Jesus seemed to be finished. I wondered if this event influenced the mother, father, and grandmother in their place in the afterlife. I had several experiences with severe anger between family members who had died, and through a family member who was alive accomplished reconciliation in a similar manner.

The patient was quite stunned and taken back by what occurred. I told the patient I would see him tomorrow after

[176]

heart surgery. The next day I got to the hospital in the afternoon, and I went to Intensive Care to check on the patient. I asked the nurse how the patient was doing, and she said "fine." She went on to say that the surgeons, prior to opening his chest to begin the heart surgery, performed a heart catheterization procedure that allowed the surgeons to see the arteries and aortic heart valve. This is a standard procedure before heart surgery and was also done two days earlier, which identified the need for surgery. They were very perplexed as there were no clogged arteries, and the patient seemed to have a new aortic heart valve. The surgeons were stunned as to why their tests seemed to be faulty. However, the man displayed none of the symptoms that brought him into the doctor.

This example of physical healing and psychological and spiritual healing is common when the senses experience the presence of Jesus, what I call an encounter with the person of Jesus. To love and to be reconciled with our sin changes the world as we know it. I suggest this prayerful vision is a good description of why the Apostle Paul tells us in Romans 6:23, "For the wages of sin is death but the gift of God is eternal life in Christ Jesus our Lord."

When I had five bypasses in 2015, I reflected on this healing but knew I was not going to be so blessed, and I underwent surgery. In 2022 I needed a new heart valve and again wondered what was going to happen; I went to surgery.

EPISODE 8
Evil

23

Satan Intrudes into my Meditation

At age 19, I experienced my great temptation while I was in the military. I spent much time meditating and learning more and more about the brain and its various functional qualities. One evening I was meditating outside on the porch. I was mentally attempting to move an object on which I was focusing, and not focusing on the divine but focusing on having power over nature. After about one hour of meditation for some reason it seemed to me that I needed assistance to move the object. This was the first time such a thought occurred to me and, in retrospect, likely from the evil one.

I had a very close relationship with my uncle and asked him to help me, even though he had been dead for several years. Almost immediately, he was standing next to me on my left side. He was communicating with me, not by words, but by feelings. The emotion I was receiving from him was a profound and deep sorrow that goes beyond what words can describe. I interpreted his feeling of sorrow as to say that I was doing something mortally wrong. By mortally wrong I mean that I was going off the path so far that getting back on the path would be very difficult. From the psychological perspective I seemed to understand that such behavior, on my part, was deadly because I was in some way supplanting the authority of the divine. In fact, my sense was that what I was doing was imposing my power over the soul of a person to make him a slave. Without freedom we cannot choose for or against the divine but only exist under the yoke of being a slave. Be that to a person, group, or ideology, it creates profound sorrow in the divine. My uncle never said a word, but his face and the emotions of sorrow were so loud that I could hear his sorrow in the depths of my soul.

At the same time another person appeared in front of me. This person had a very dark face and body. It was very strange as I could see him very clearly, but it was as if no light was being reflected off him. My uncle was bright, not glowing, but illuminated as if light was shining on him. The person standing in front of me didn't have dark skin, but no light reflected from him, as if any light was being completely absorbed by him. He also was clothed in a hooded robe of some sort. I could see the features of the person in front of me, but it was like looking at death. My uncle's face was alive but this other person's face was death. In my soul I knew the person was Satan. He was standing 12 inches in front of me, nose to nose. He said to me, "I will give you what you want if you worship me." My response to him was immediate. "I have chosen to serve God and him alone." After I said that my uncle's sorrow turned to a joyful heart. I asked for my uncle's forgiveness and while he never responded to me, I knew that I was reconciled with my uncle and with God, and my uncle left. Satan just disappeared and I was alone.

After the event, it seemed to me, to be like Satan's temptation of Jesus. I am not suggesting that my encounter with Satan is equal to Jesus's but when I told Satan that I serve my Father, and he alone, Satan left. This told me that Satan has no power. For me this insight is very important,

[182]

and I would always remember that the only power evil has is the power we give to evil, allowing me not to be afraid when confronted by evil. But there is one thing that Satan, or evil has no control over, and that is human free will. From my perspective the difference between Satan and the condition is free will versus slavery, which is the hallmark of Evil.

For several years I reflected on my spontaneous response, "I have chosen to serve God and him alone," and in 1954 my spontaneous response, "I dedicate my life to God." I also reflected on what it meant: I will give you what you want. For a long time, I thought it meant moving an object, but I have come to realize that moving an object is like having power over someone and thus making them a slave, which was the origin of my uncle's sorrow. For me this was a great lesson on humility and how to deal with those around me without attempting to make anyone my slave. It is very difficult to pull off because we are very subtle about the way we try to control others, most of the time from what we believe to be for good reasons. What Satan was going to give me was power over people to make them a slave to evil. This is the same thing that occurs with law, dogma, and ideologies as they focus on enslaving others. He was offering me discipleship.

This event taught me not to be afraid of Satan, his angels, or the fruit of his hands. He has no power of his own. He gets his power from those who he deludes, deceives, lies to, or imitates what they think is his power. This left me with many questions. How do people become possessed? How does he gain or use power? What does this have to do with salvation? Why did he come to me when I wasn't asking for him? Why did he leave once I said I would not worship him? Did my uncle see him? The universe is very mysterious, more than we fully realize.

[183]

I also seem to know why in scripture Jesus had no personal concerns when confronting or being confronted by Satan or his angels. I also have had several encounters with evil during my ministry. This experience with Satan gave me insights into who and what he is and how he functions. It isn't Satan to fear, provided we are dedicated to God. No, it isn't Satan but those who are his slaves. If Satan had the power people claim he has, then Satan would have taken control over the entire world many milieus ago. He is deceitful, cunning and knows only how to lie. He traps people to be under his influence by treachery and in modernity he uses laws, dogmas, and ideologies as his favorite way to bring people into his fold. It was important for my Father to allow me to encounter the persona of evil because many years later I would put what he taught me to good use.

For many years I was greatly troubled by this event and wondered if it was an aspect of my instinct of evil in the form of the person of Satan or perhaps some aspect of my imagination. But over time, and my experiences of encountering evil over many years, and how I responded to evil, confirm to me that my instinctual identification of the person as being Satan was correct. I was always told that Satan has great power, but my experience confirms he is powerless and only achieves power through others. This conclusion left me with more questions. What types of power do humans have? If Satan has all this power that it is claimed he has, why doesn't he control the soul of every person? Why do people choose to associate with Satan or better, evil? Why have my experiences with evil seemed to indicate that I have more power than Satan and why is it I choose not to use it indiscriminately? There are so many questions that I cannot lay them all out.

[184]

I have concluded why Jesus was unafraid of demons and the like in Scripture. I believe it was because of his encounter with Satan in the wilderness when he fasted for 40 days in preparation for his public ministry. He realized that Satan has no power of his own but steals it from people who are enslaved to him via deceitful and cunning lies. This realization is what allowed me to never be concerned when facing some form of evil, and why my encounters with evil were always peaceful.

24

I Terrified a Person in Jail

A deacon friend called and told me about a person in the county jail who he visited several times but had the suspicion he was oppressed or possessed by an evil spirit. After discussing the behaviors, I agreed to accompany him on his next visit.

The prisoner was told that I would be joining the deacon, and the person said that it was okay for me to come with him. We went into the visiting room before the person we were visiting entered. Then the person came in and when the person saw me, he panicked, and immediately backed up into a corner of the room near the door, getting as far away from me as possible. The prisoner only said, "Why are you here?" I did not respond as several guards rushed in to get the person out of the visiting room. Strange thing for them to say as they knew I was coming with my deacon friend and knew I too was a deacon. The deacon said to me, "I guess I have my answer." The next day the person was transferred to one of the state prisons and the deacon never saw him again.

I have revealed this event as an example of how people seem to see me as someone who can see into their soul. One of the reasons, I believe, is why people are uncomfortable being around me. For several years I would fly between

Denver and Las Vegas several times a month. I would always sit in the same row, same side of the plane, and next to the window. After at least 60 flights I never had anyone sit next to me. Only several times did I have a person sit in the aisle seat once, and on one occasion the plane was full, and the only seat left was next to me, it was the last seat filled. This harkens back to what the hospital staff member said, "Do you know why you have no social encounters with the staff?"

25

The Boy with Glowing Eyes

Shortly after being ordained, my pastor sent me to visit a family who told the pastor their son, who was 14 years old, was acting strange and seemingly embracing evil through the friends he had and that they were into drugs and the drug culture. Their son was talking about worshipping Satan and his friends were participating in worship services to evil. The family went to Mass weekly, but their son wasn't interested in participating in the Mass as he once was. His brothers and sisters were also becoming afraid of him because at times in the night his eyes glowed red and they wanted him and the house exorcised.

My pastor called me and asked me to bless the house and assess the situation. He thought it would be good for me to experience such things as they occur from time to time. I called and set an appointment to meet with the family in the evening when everyone was at home. As this was my first encounter with such a request, I really didn't know what to make of it. So, in my prayers before going I reflected on my encounter with Satan while I was in the Air Force and remembered that Satan had no power of his own and that he gains power by inciting fear which separates one from God.

My prayer and reflection gave me a sense of peace about going into such a situation for the first time.

I met with the family several days later, arriving just after the sun went down. I was welcomed and we sat down in the living room, but their son was downstairs in his bedroom. After prompting their son to join us, he finally did, and we talked for a short time to allow me to get a sense of his spiritual condition or well-being. It was not good. I sensed he had opened his heart to evil. After my assessment I decided it was time to go into his room. I wanted to go into the basement where his bedroom was, by myself. The mother showed me the door to the basement and where the light was, but I told her I wanted to go without the lights. She was surprised and commented that they don't go down there without the lights anymore. I assured her it was okay.

I went down the stairs, and then asked her to close the door to reduce any light illuminating the basement. It made it easier for my eyes to adjust to the darkness. I spent a few minutes getting a spiritual sense of his space and the rest of the basement area. I felt there was an evil presence, and it was centered in the corner of the basement to the right side of the stairs. I used my hands to feel my way around and felt that the central heating furnace was in the center of the basement and the evil presence was to the right of it. I focused on that area of the basement and prayed for Jesus to bless that area and to place angels to protect that space from evil. The evil seemed to leave, and I felt a sense of peace. I continued to feel my way around working my way back to the stairs. I blessed the basement with holy water, then went up to meet with the family. They too said that they felt a sense of peace that they hadn't felt for a long time.

We talked for a while, and I focused on their son to see how he was doing, and he seemed better. I then said I would like to bless the house and each person, and they agreed, even their son. I blessed each room and then we went down into the basement, this time with the lights. It was a mess, and like most basements became a place for all sorts of things. His bed and space were in the far corner where I felt negative energy but didn't feel it anymore. The family, except the son, all commented that the basement was much more peaceful. Then I blessed each person while we were in the basement. I never saw that the eyes of the boy glowed as the parent reported but when they saw the pastor later, they said their son was back to his old self and was no longer associating with those who were leading him down the wrong path. My report to the pastor was that I blessed the house and the family, and I think all is well.

26

The Young Girl with Evil Spirits

In this example a young girl's reality was infused with religious ideology (which is nearly always the case), and all of it was done unconsciously except when the person was experiencing the effects of an altered reality but would have no idea the cause. I also use this event to demonstrate how judgment on others, if unreconciled, will create a form of punishment that will either affect the person's physical body, their emotions or psyche and in this case their spirit.

An 11-year-old girl was experiencing two evil spirits. The girl's mother took her to their medical doctor and to a psychologist who were unable to do anything for her. The mother then took her to the priest at her parish who was unable to help, and he suggested they see me. The mother and father were beside themselves because over the course of about four years the girl went from being afraid to be in her bedroom (because she thought there was someone in the room with her) to having black beings emerging out of the floor about three feet at the foot of her bed. Eventually these black beings would come up to the side of the bed as if they were going to take her down into the holes from which they emerged. The parents were unable to see anything that their daughter said was haunting her.

The mother brought her to see me and after listening to the problem I asked them what her relationship was with the members of the family. She said how much she loved her family. I sensed that there was an evil presence with her and so I wasn't interested in counseling as others had already attempted that course of action. I believed this to be a spiritual issue and needed to be dealt with through prayer. I asked if it was okay if we prayed, and the mother said yes. I sensed that she made an inappropriate judgment and God wanted to heal her but would have to forgive those who hurt her.

The young girl's mother remained in the office with us, and we began to pray. I asked her to close her eyes and ask Jesus to come to her. She closed her eyes and in a very short time Jesus appeared to her in her mind and to me in my mind but not the young girl's mother. I have never understood or figured out how it is possible for me to see what is happening in another person's mind but could see and hear what she saw and heard. While we were praying and without asking, the two dark beings were standing in front of her, and to me they looked very evil, threatening, and were featureless other than their dark or black clothing that looked like robes, resembling the person of Satan. She verified these were the spirits that would come out of the floor to torment her and tried to torment her while we were in prayer by accusing her of judging her mother, father, and sister. By accusing her while in prayer the evil within her wanted to stop her from becoming reconciled with her parents.

Some part of her emotional system hated her parents, and beings were accusing her before God and demanding he judge her and punish her. I was surprised that even with Jesus standing next to the girl the evil beings were very near to her acting in the manner they did when they would come out of the floor. Jesus didn't exorcise the evil beings, which greatly surprised me. It was as if Jesus was the observer of what was occurring, and it was up to me to set her free from evil, and I knew that the young girl would have to forgive from her own free will. I asked her who each of the spirits were. It took a while, but she said they were her parents who she hated for not allowing her to go with her sister to an event she wanted to go to some years ago. Around the same time, she began to be afraid in her room. Now it was up to her to forgive her parents and older sister freely and completely.

Besides disliking her mother and father for not allowing her to go, she distrusted her mother and father because they were unable to protect her from these evil beings; this was a no-win situation for the parents. In the prayer the image of the mother and father were present in the form of evil spirits that were full of her emotional vitriol. The fact that there were only two evil spirits indicated to me that her sister was not being judged to the same degree. All this seemed to have occurred when she was about the age of seven years old. She had a severe case of "feeling sorry for herself" that resulted in emotionally making her the center of the universe, a sin against the divine who is just not the center of the universe but is all there is in the universe. "Feeling sorry for herself" created enough psychic energy to become embedded into her emotional system. This energy was triggered by anger that prompted her survival mechanism into a "flight or fight" mode. She chose to run, and the enormous psychic energy that was released created "two evil spirits" to exact punishment for the judgment on her parents.

I want to note that when we have evil beings in our psyche, even when we are unaware of them, they are generally created out of unreconciled judgments that are

[193]

energized by anger. We also see that these evil spirits stand before God and accuse those with whom we are unreconciled as being the one responsible for the problem and that God should punish them. We emotionally, meaning psychologically, punish ourselves either physically, emotionally, or spiritually. The reason we perceive that God should punish those with whom we are angry is, if God punishes them, we are right in our judgment. But God will never judge them because He will not validate a sin as being good; it would be a lie. The sin is in the judgment, regardless of what is inflicted on a person. Even though Jesus was falsely accused, tried, and crucified, Jesus did not judge them, nor did he want his Father to judge them, "Forgive them Father, for they don't know what they are doing." (Luke 23:34)

The girl was confronted with her judgments against her parents by Jesus and through Jesus was able to forgive. When Jesus is present, love is immeasurable, and forgiveness is so much easier. This is why I advocate praying in a manner that allows for a personal encounter with Jesus. Her forgiveness was validated by the young girl being able to embrace her mother and father in the vision. Jesus now told the evil beings to return to their hole in the ground and they did, meaning that she no longer had a need to feel guilty for her judgment, for from within her emotional system it never happened. I asked the young girl to see her guardian angel, which she did, and to ask him to stand over two holes in front of her bed and not allow the evil spirits out of the ground. This entire session lasted about one and a half hours. The girl never had another experience of evil beings and her relationship with her mother and father greatly improved, as well as with her sister.

Were these evil spirits or just her imagination? The answer is yes to both possibilities. Are they evil spirits as beings following Satan? Yes. But most occasions of evil are created by our judgments that become the vehicle of our punishment. Healing occurs when we authentically become reconciled with the sin of our judgments.

27

The Woman whose Heart Stopped
Three Times

This took place while at work as a chaplain. A patient was brought to the emergency room by the police who found her nearly unconscious from drugs. She had no family or ID and was homeless. After being medically stabilized, she was transferred to intensive care before being sent for psychological evaluation the next day in our psych ward. The doctors wanted to monitor her heart and her blood levels for drugs to make sure she would be well enough to be transferred to the psych ward in the morning. I went to intensive care to check on the patient, and as I walked by her room, she saw me and knew I was a cleric because of my Roman collar. The nurse was with her, so I did not go in to see her. She was transferred from the emergency room about five hours earlier and was doing very well, presenting no behavioral or medical problems, and interacting with her nurse and medical staff appropriately.

I recognized she was the only new patient as I knew the others, and I wanted to talk to her later after the new shift completed their reports regarding anything that needed to be done. I began to visit with a doctor friend of mine who was seeing one of his patients. After about ten minutes the woman who I was going to see later, suddenly sat up in bed and began shouting and cursing while at the same time throwing anything she could out of the room. Three nurses quickly responded and when they entered the room the woman's heart stopped; a sudden "flat line." A COR-O team was called a medical emergency that a patient's heart had stopped. The COR-O team responded quickly to resuscitate her. The nurses began compressions on her heart while the entire COR-O team was arriving. They proceeded to follow normal protocol with no response. I was a member of the COR-O team to take care of the spiritual needs of the patient, family, and staff, and would wait until the entire medical team were in their places in the room before I joined them to avoid being in the way.

The doctor I was chatting with was not involved, as the patient wasn't his and the COR-O team has a doctor specific to this type of medical emergency. I told the doctor that I had a feeling that this COR-O team was going to be more my job than the medical team's job. He looked at me as if I was a little off. It was as if Jesus was telling me this was a spiritual issue. I had attended several thousand COR-O teams during the time I was a chaplain but never had the feeling I was going to be the one who brought the person back to life. I also felt the presence of evil spirits close by, which was why I felt this person's heart stopping was a spiritual issue and was not going to be resolved by medical intervention.

The COR-O team assembled and worked on the woman but without her heart responding to their efforts. I told my doctor friend that it was time for me to go in, and this was going to be interesting. I went to the patient's room and stood by the door. I did not go in, hoping she would respond, but her heart would not respond to the treatment. I

[197]

stepped into the room and the woman's heart immediately began to beat normally as if nothing had happened. Medical intervention was suspended because her heart had a normal rhythm. I felt, however, this was only the beginning, and she was still in danger. I stepped out of the room and as I did, the woman's heart stopped again. As the first time, there was an immediate flat line. The COR-O team reacted quickly to her medical condition and resumed resuscitating her, again without a positive response. I had the sense she was possessed by evil spirits that were trying to kill her.

I stood by the door looking into the room and the COR-O team all looked at me as if to see what I was going to do. I stepped into the room and her heart started to beat with a normal rhythm. The patient remained unconscious, her heart had a normal rhythm and so again I stepped out of the room. Just as before, her heart stopped beating. I waited outside the patient's room and the COR-O team had their eyes on me, waiting to see what I was going to do. So, for the third time I stepped into the room and the patient's heart began to beat with a normal heart rhythm, but this time the patient woke up and was fully conscious. The staff moved away allowing me to walk over to her side and she said, "They are trying to kill me." I told her, "I know they are." Now the feeling of an evil presence was very strong, and I could sense that there were two demons that had been tormenting her for most of her life; she was about 35 years old. I told her I have driven them out of your life and God has forgiven you. They will never attack you again. I also sensed the presence of Jesus and that's how I knew her sins were forgiven. That is what he does; he forgives us our sins and leads us to the Father by helping us to get back on the path. It was Jesus who was answering a poor soul's long-standing prayer, who healed her body, her mind, and her spirit. I was fortunate to be there to witness his eternal love

[198]

in action. It was Jesus that saved her from the slavery or bondage of evil. I was with her for less than one minute. It doesn't take very long for Jesus to work a miracle.

The staff were acutely watching me, and you could see on their faces they were perplexed and did not say anything to me for fear that their own sins would be revealed to them. As I was getting ready to leave the room, I stopped before going out of the room and told the doctor that she was okay now and she would have no further medical issues or even drug issues. Everyone was waiting to see what would happen when I left the room. I stepped out of the room and the woman was fine; however, I don't think the medical team was okay. They didn't know what to do with what they just witnessed. I went back to the doctor I was chatting with, and he said, "that was the damnedest thing I have ever seen." The woman was discharged from the hospital the next day instead of being transferred for a psychological evaluation. There was no evidence that her heart had ever stopped multiple times.

I did not see her again that night because of other pressing issues I was called to deal with but planned on seeing her in the psych ward the next day. When I checked on her, I was informed that she had no medical issues, there was no trace of drugs in her body, and no evidence that her heart stopped three times. She was released from the hospital that morning, leaving the medical staff perplexed. The woman returned to the hospital about a month later looking for me to thank me and tell me that she was free from what she called her demons and use of drugs. Thanks be to God, and his love and desire to save.

28

Steps for having a Lived Encounter
with Jesus

Praying like this is difficult. You must be patient and determined. Four reasons why such prayer is so difficult.

The primary reason is that we have accepted laws, dogmas, and ideologies that tell us we cannot see Jesus while we are alive. That is not true.

The second reason is that we become distracted very easily because of worldly concerns.

Thirdly, we don't meditate or pray like this and so we are just very weak at it, but we can overcome this with practice and determination.

Finally, and most critical, is because of the sins we have. It isn't the sins in themselves but that we have failed to forgive those who have sinned against us, we are emotionally wounded, or even disappointed by someone. Remember, forgive us our trespasses as we forgive those who trespass against us.

One other point -- fasting is a good way to focus on your objective, which is Jesus. There are many ways to fast and whatever helps you to focus is beneficial.

1.   Go to a quiet place, pray for about 15 minutes asking God to open your heart to become aware of one or two

specific sins that was committed against you, but no more than one or two.

If possible, allow the wound of how you were hurt to be relived, regardless of the emotional pain.

2.   Then begin to pray for those or the one who wounded you asking God's blessings on them. Sometimes it is helpful to pray a brief prayer and then follow it by asking God's blessing and you bless them as well.

Example: Father, I hold before you, (insert the name or situation) and I acknowledge how much they hurt me by (insert the behavior or action that wounded you). I ask for your spirit of love for this person (or situation) for I know you love them equally as much as you love me. Bless (the person or situation) and forgive them for any sin they have committed, as I bless and forgive them or the situation.

This should be the focus of your prayer time for at least 30 minutes after coming to recognize your own woundedness. It is important not to ask that God forgive you, at least not at this point, this is about you forgiving those who have wronged and hurt you. God forgives in accordance with your forgiveness. Pray this way daily or, if possible, two times a day until you can recollect the wound and/or the situation without experiencing the emotional pain that you once did.

3.   When you attempt to come into the presence of Jesus, prayer should be started after you have prayed as noted above. It isn't necessary to wait until you have completely forgiven, as above, but pray only after your prayer for

forgiveness. Fix your desire to be with Jesus by closing your eyes and saying quietly in your mind, "Jesus, Lord Jesus, have mercy on me a sinner." Repeat this over and over in your mind. Or, you can just say, "Jesus" repeatedly. While you are repeating this mantra, with your eyes closed, look for Jesus coming to you. He may just be standing in front of you, or you might see him walking towards you. When you see him, it is important to follow your instincts about how you interact with him, but, if possible, try to hold his hand so that you feel the warmth of his hand. This will be helpful at overcoming the natural tendency to discount the encounter after it is over. When your senses tell you that something is real, it is real. Jesus may reopen a wound that you have by somebody sinning against you. Jesus will guide you towards reconciliation. Jesus will heal you as you need healing, only God knows what you need to be healed. Encounters with the divine is always about reconciliation, first with others and then with our Father. We cannot be reconciled with God when we have not forgiven those who have wounded us for God loves all people equally, even the worst sinner that ever lived. He cherishes free will and will always allow us to come to Him. If unsuccessful in seeing Jesus, try, try again.

4.   In the gospel of Luke 18:35 ff, and in Mark10:46 ff, is the healing of the blind man, Bartimaeus, on the road to Jericho. This is a wonderful image in which to place yourself by becoming the one being healed. Note that persistence is important. It is also important to recognize our sinfulness and desire to be forgiven as well as healed. This is the scripture that "Jesus, son of David, have mercy on me" comes from, and is helpful to say while praying.

My prayer for you: May our Father open your eyes to know his infinite love for you and may you set your heart on the forgiveness of those who have hurt you and our Father will forgive you the sins that separate you from him. God bless you and your family, extended family, and all your ancestors.